The World's
MOST
FANTASTIC
FREAKS

The World's
MOST
FANTASTIC
FREAKS

Mike Parker

OCTOPUS BOOKS

**First published in hardback in 1983
by Octopus Books Limited
59 Grosvenor Street
London W1**

Paperback edition first published in 1984

© Octopus Books Limited

ISBN 0 7064 2145 0

Second impression, reprinted 1984

Made and printed in Great Britain by
Richard Clay (The Chaucer Press) Limited
Bungay, Suffolk

Contents

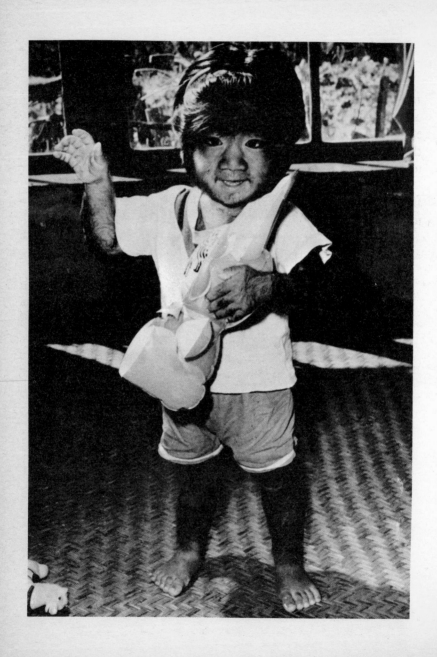

Introduction

They are loved, loathed, feared, despised and even worshipped; human beings whose appearances and natures often conspire to defy that very description. We call them freaks. We have exhibited them, exploited them, applauded them, laughed at them and, sometimes, shut them far away from the world.

But human beings they are. The short, the tall, the fat, the thin, the mighty, the feeble, the grotesque and the downright outrageous; people thrust into a prying, probing limelight because they are different.

Yet what lies behind the peep show curtains? Behind the sober, medical textbooks and the screaming newspaper headlines? Since history began to be chronicled, no-one has captured public curiosity in all its manifestations of emotion as much as the human freak. Here are the stories of those people – men and women far from the ordinary – who are The World's Greatest Freaks.

Chapter One

Freaks of Face and Figure

The Elephant Man

'**S**tand up!' The penny showman barked his command. And from a darkened corner of the room, what had appeared to be a pile of filthy rags began to stir. Slowly, an inhuman-looking shape began to rise in the gloom, discarding the tattered blanket under which it had cowered. A stench of decaying fruit filled the air as the figure laboured to pull itself to the limit of its bowed height.

Joseph Carey Merrick finally stood quite still. In the dimness of the old shop, once used by a greengrocer, he cast a strange, unnerving shadow; a hideous, nightmarish caricature of a human being, or of something only half-human. He appeared to have the legs and body of a man. But his head, face and one arm were so grotesquely distorted that they seemed to represent the profile of a wild beast with a long, pendulous trunk. Joseph Merrick, the wretched, stooping, sideshow attraction in the hired shop at No. 123 Whitechapel Road, London, was the Elephant Man.

Outside the shop, opposite the famous London Hospital, a garish, painted poster advertised the most famous of all freaks exhibited in sensation-hungry Victorian England. And such was Merrick's monstrous appeal that his penny showman master was able to charge a handsome tuppence-a-peep at his prize specimen. The Elephant Man was big business.

In 1884 a young and ambitious surgeon from the London Hospital crossed the road one day to investigate beyond the lurid poster which had caught his eye from an upper window. Frederick – later to become Sir Frederick – Treves, wrote of the freakshow billboard:

'This very crude production depicted a frightful creature that could only have been possible in a nightmare. It was the figure of a man with the characteristics of an elephant. The transfiguration was not far advanced. There was still more of the man than of the beast. This fact – that it was still human – was the most repellent attribute of the creature. There was nothing about it of the pitiableness of the misshapened or the deformed, nothing of the grotesqueness of the freak, but merely the loathing insinuation of a man being changed into an animal. Some palm trees in the background of the picture suggested a jungle and might have led the imagination to assume that it was in this wild that the perverted object had roamed.'

Inside the shop Treves caught his first sight of the Elephant Man. The pathetic Merrick, then aged 21, was stripped naked to the waist, bare-footed and wearing only a ragged pair of trousers several sizes too large for him. A hip disease had left him lame and he was only able to stand upright using a

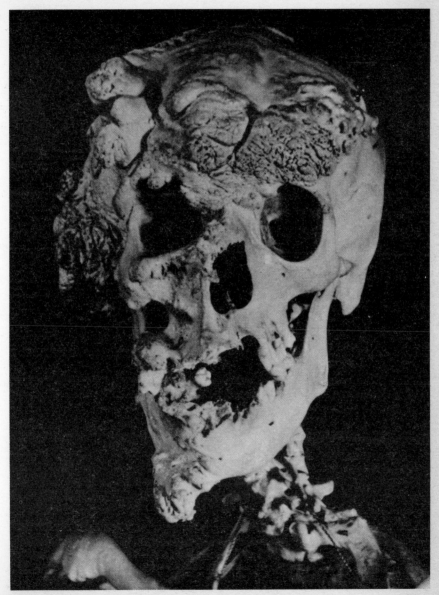

Joseph Merrick's deformed skull

stick. A huge, bony growth had enlarged his head to the thickness of a man's waist, almost hiding one eye, and a second gnarled growth had twisted his mouth into a trunk-like shape. Treves described the face as totally expressionless and wooden, like an ugly native idol. Both legs and one arm were swollen, misshapen and useless, ending in hands and feet no better than paddles, with fat, stunted fingers and toes. In stark contrast, one arm was perfectly formed with smooth skin and a delicate, sensitive hand. A colleague of Treves later said of Merrick: 'The poor fellow . . . was deformed in body, face, head and limbs. His skin, thick and pendulous, hung in folds and resembled the hide of an elephant – hence his show name.'

Little is known of the early life of Merrick, who seemed to have appeared from nowhere as a freak-show horror in London's East End. According to his birth certificate, however, he was born on 5 August 1862, the son of Joseph Rockley Merrick and Mary Jane Merrick, at 50 Lee Street, Leicester. His mother was a cripple, the family home was a slum and, shortly after his birth, Joseph Merrick was abandoned to an orphanage. For as long as he could remember, he had been exhibited as a freak, passing from one keeper to another and from one peepshow to the next. He could speak, but his appalling facial deformities made his words barely intelligible.

The only life he had ever known was in a fairground booth as an object of derision, revulsion or sneering humour; so near to the laughing, cringing crowds to whom he was forced to display his body, yet so far removed from a normal existence. It is known that Merrick could read, but the only books he was ever given were a bible and cheap romantic novels. He was childlike, naive about worldly matters. His idea of pleasure was to lock himself away in a shuttered room.

After much persuasion, Treves managed to prise the Elephant Man away from his keeper. Showman Tom Norman agreed to allow the surgeon to examine him. The examination took place – but just 24 hours later police closed the Whitechapel Road show and Merrick and Norman vanished. Merrick fled to the continent and a string of new masters. But in towns all over Europe, exhibitions of the Elephant Man were being banned and censured as being degrading. Eventually, in Brussels, he ceased to be a viable asset. His latest master robbed him of his savings, gave him a railway ticket to London and washed his hands of him. Merrick was alone, unwanted and penniless; a bizarre, cloaked figure who hid his face with a huge cap pulled well down to avoid investigation by suspicious and untrusting strangers.

Treves, in an essay on the life of the Elephant Man, wrote of Merrick's voyage home: 'The journey may be imagined. Merrick was in his alarming outdoor garb. He would be harried by an eager mob as he hobbled along the quay. They would run ahead to get a look at him. They would lift the hem of

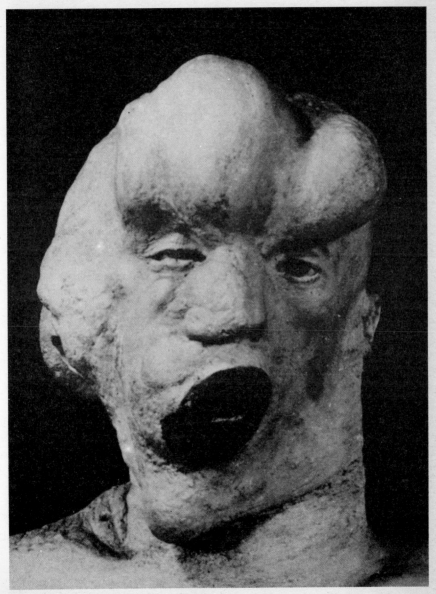

Reconstruction of the Elephant Man's face

his cloak to peep at his body. He would try to hide in the train or in some dark corner of the boat, but never could be free from that ring of curious eyes or from those whispers of fright and aversion. He had but a few shillings in his pocket and nothing to eat or drink on the way. A panic-dazed dog with a label on his collar would have received some sympathy and possibly some kindness. Merrick received none.'

Somehow, amazingly, Merrick managed to make it to London's Liverpool Street Station, where he was found, terrified, exhausted and huddled in the darkest corner of the waiting room, by a policeman. He was clutching his only remaining possession – Frederick Treves' business card. Treves was called for, and was able to usher the creature he immediately recognized through a gawping crowd and into a cab to the London Hospital. There he hoped to provide a permanent refuge for Merrick, despite a hospital rule against taking chronic or incurable cases. Treves succeeded in persuading the hospital's management committee to make an exception, and so began the second life of the Elephant Man.

In a letter to the *Times* newspaper, the hospital management committee immediately launched a public appeal for funds. Within a week, enough money had been raised to keep Merrick there for the rest of his life. A self-contained suite of two isolation rooms was allocated to him. Treves was now able to begin the long and arduous task of trying to rehabilitate him. Slowly, he learned to understand Merrick's speech. And then he made a discovery which was to add a new, tragic twist. In most cases of such extreme physical deformity, Treves believed, there was an accompanying lack of intelligence and understanding which helped lessen the subject's awareness of his appearance. In Merrick's case, he had been blessed – or perhaps cursed – with a sensitive, intelligent mind, fully aware of his appearance and desperate for affection.

Treves wrote: 'Those who are interested in the evolution of character might speculate as to the effect of this brutish life upon a sensitive and intelligent man. It would be reasonable to surmise that he would become a spiteful and malignant misanthrope, swollen with venom and filled with hatred of his fellow men, or, on the other hand, that he would degenerate into a despairing melancholic on the verge of idiocy. Merrick, however, was no such being. He had passed through the fire and had come out unscathed. His troubles had ennobled him. He showed himself to be a gentle, affectionate and lovable creature ... free from any trace of cynicism or resentment, without a grievance and without an unkind word for anyone. I have never heard him deplore his ruined life or resent the treatment he had received at the hands of callous keepers. His gratitude to those about him was pathetic in its sincerity and eloquent in the childlike simplicity with which it was expressed.'

Gradually, under the care of Treves, Merrick progressed. Yet he remained haunted by one nagging doubt. He could not understand, or believe, that his stay at the London Hospital was to be permanent. 'When am I going to be moved?' he asked Treves, 'and where to?' Pathetically, he asked that if he had to be moved, could it be to a lighthouse, or an asylum for the blind, where at least he would be free from the ridicule of his fellow men. Slowly, Merrick's health began to improve and his confidence grew daily. 'I am happier every hour of the day,' he told Treves, an expression of joy which prompted the gifted surgeon to try a further experiment.

Treves persuaded a young lady friend to visit Merrick and spend some time talking with him. The girl agreed. As she walked into Merrick's room, she smiled and held out her hand. Merrick bowed his heavy head and wept. His tears, though, were not in sadness. He was still a young man of only 23, with a tender feeling for anything beautiful. And it was the first time in his life that a beautiful woman had smiled at him, or even taken his hand.

That poignant moment proved to be another turning point in Merrick's life. His fame began to spread far beyond the hospital walls and many people became eager to meet the celebrated Elephant Man. They were allowed to do so, provided they behaved as guests and not sensation-seeking sightseers. Soon, Merrick's hospital suite was decorated with signed pictures of Victorian socialites who flocked to see him. But his greatest joy was still to come . . .

It came on the day he was visited by his most important guest, the Princess of Wales (later Queen Alexandra). She made a special visit to take tea with Merrick. That visit was the first of many, and Treves later wrote of the Elephant Man's Royal appointments:

'The Queen . . . sent him every year a Christmas card with a message in her own handwriting. On one occasion she sent him a signed photograph of herself. Merrick, quite overcome, regarded it as a sacred object and would hardly allow me to touch it. He cried over it, and after it was framed had it put up in his room as a kind of icon. I told him that he must write to Her Royal Highness to thank her for her goodness. This he was pleased to do, as he was very fond of writing letters, never before in his life having had anyone to write to. I allowed the letter to be dispatched unedited. It began "My dear Princess" and ended "Yours very sincerely". Unorthodox as it was, it was expressed in terms any courtier would have envied.'

As the Elephant Man's life began to blossom, there were, more and more frequently, expeditions outside the hospital. A famous actress of the period arranged a private box for him at the Drury Lane Theatre, where Merrick was allowed to use the Royal entrance. There, with a screen of nurses in evening dress in front of him, Merrick watched, transfixed, as a troupe of pantomime players took to the stage. He was deeply impressed, if confused. It did not occur to him that the performances he was watching were not part of real life. Long after his visit, he spoke of the characters portrayed as if they were real people and as if the show he had seen was still going on.

Once, he was allowed to visit Treves' own home, where he gaped in astonishment at every room. He had read descriptions of furniture-filled homes, but he had never been inside a real house. The safe refuge of a gamekeeper's lodge was also found, so that Merrick could enjoy trips to the country. Peeping from a freak show caravan on his earlier travels, he had often seen trees and fields, but he had never before actually walked in a wood, or picked a flower. Merrick's stay in the country became an immensely happy period in his life. He wrote to Treves in ecstasy, enclosing daisies, dandelions and buttercups; simple flowers, but to him rare and beautiful objects. In his letters, Merrick told how he had seen strange birds, startled a hare from her form, made friends with a fierce dog and watched trout darting in a stream.

After a few weeks in the country, Merrick returned to the hospital, happy to be 'home' with his personal possessions. More and more he tried to become like other human beings. But his deformities, if anything, became worse. A report later revealed his continuing tragedy:

'The bony masses and pendulous flaps of skin grew steadily. The outgrowths from the upper jaw and its integuments – the so-called trunk – increased so as to render his speech more and more difficult to understand. The most serious feature, however, in the patient's illness was the increasing size of the head ... The head grew so heavy that at length he had great difficulty in holding it up. He slept in a sitting or crouching position, with his hands clasped over his legs and his head on his knees. If he lay down flat the heavy head tended to fall back and produce a sense of suffocation.'

One night in April 1890, Joseph Carey Merrick, the Elephant Man, was found dead in his bed. He died because of his desperate desire to be like other people. And, in a desperate, fateful last experiment, he tried to sleep flat on his back.

After Merrick's death, it was Treves's painful duty to dissect the Elephant Man's body and eventually remount his bones into the appallingly misshapen skeleton which remains today. It must have been an agonizing task for the skilled surgeon, who had grown so close to his strange patient. Yet, of the man he once described as 'the most disgusting specimen of humanity' that he had ever seen, Treves was finally to write this epitaph:

'As a specimen of humanity, Merrick was ignoble and repulsive; but the spirit of Merrick, if it could be seen in the form of the living, would assume the figure of an upstanding and heroic man, smooth browed and clean of limb ... and with eyes that flashed undaunted courage.'

Yellow look

The great Emperor Napoleon was said on occasions to become so fierce that a single glance from him could wither a man to terrible discomfort. What perhaps is more likely to have startled the victims of his wrath, however, was the fact that the whites of his eyes were not white at all, but of a shining, strangely luminous yellow tint.

The Elephant Boy

A smash-hit film about the Elephant Man threw fresh misery into the life of little Tony Albarran. It gave mocking playmates, who already called him a monster, a cruel new name to taunt him with: the Elephant Boy.

For Tony, aged 4, one glance in the mirror confirmed his resemblance to the face in the movie; by a tragic twist of fate he appeared to be a child-parody of the hideously disfigured Victorian freak. His features were swollen and misshapen by a rare disease which causes huge tumours to erupt all over the body. His forehead, left eye, chin, nose and mouth and even his gums and tongue were horribly distorted by the agonizing growths which made it difficult for him to eat, sleep and, sometimes, breathe.

Heartbreak followed heartbreak as Tony's parents took him to specialist after specialist in their home city of Chicago. He did undergo vital surgery to remove the largest lumps from his forehead and correct problems in his left eye. But doctors insisted that a major operation to cut away one enormous tumour which threatened to engulf his face would be too dangerous.

Tony's father, Hector Albarran, said: 'He would stand in front of a mirror tearing at the lumpy flesh. We couldn't let him play with other kids because they tormented him. I knew that if we didn't do something soon, his body and mind would be permanently affected by his bizarre disease. It was terrible. For us every moment of little Tony's existence, looking as he did, was sheer agony. I knew that if we waited much longer he would never have a chance to live a normal life. I felt something needed to be done right away before the tumour destroyed his face.'

As each day passed, Tony's features grew more distorted, pressed into wild shapes by the lumps that continued to sprout. At times, he cried out in pain when the suffocating force of the eruptions became unbearable. Virtually all his friends deserted him and the playmates who remained stayed only to tease and taunt. Tony's parents recall the deep shame he confessed to feeling as his condition worsened. And still, no doctor would agree to free the little boy from his torment.

The first ray of hope did arrive, however, in January 1982, when Dr Kenneth Salyer, a leading plastic surgeon from the Children's Medical Centre in Dallas, Texas, agreed to examine Tony. And, finally, to Tony's parent's immense relief, he decided that the Elephant Boy was a suitable case for treatment. At last their son would have the chance to live as a normal, healthy child.

In a series of delicate operations, Dr Salyer began to remove layer after layer of the lumpy tissue which gave Tony's face its elephantine appearance. In the first week of January alone, little Tony spent six hours on the operating table. Dr Salyer had consented to commence surgery even though the boy's parents didn't have enough money to pay him immediately.

Gradually, Tony's face began to appear smoother, his features more clearly contoured and defined. Yet there was still so much growth that initially, Dr Salyer was only able to remove part of it. As the operations continued, he developed a 'whittling-away' process, at first working on the outside of Tony's face and then cutting away the ugly growths which had sprouted inside his mouth, pulling even his tongue and gums out of shape and at times making it virtually impossible to eat properly.

By the end of February, despite a slightly puffy, swollen look, Tony's face was near-normal. The heartbreak, it seemed, was over – apart from one final complication. According to Dr Salyer, the tumours will begin to re-grow on Tony's face and he will have to undergo future operations to cut them away before they have a chance to mushroom again.

Meanwhile, though, little Tony's ecstasy is reflected not only in the mirror into which he now looks with pride, but also in the words of his father, who says: 'His life as an Elephant Boy is over. I know he'll be all right now, even though he'll need other operations. He's not shy any more and he even keeps pestering us to let him go outside and play with the other kids. Every time I look at him I can't believe our good fortune. My dear little Tony isn't a freak any more – and at last he'll have a chance to lead a normal life.'

After a short life filled with pain and shame, the torment of a film which helped brand him the Elephant Boy and a desperate, year-long search for a doctor who would end his misery, little Tony himself says, with the simple innocence of a child: 'I feel better now. My face doesn't hurt at night and I don't look so funny.'

Ugliest man

John Heidegger earned himself a title that would make the self-conscious collapse with embarrassment: the 'Ugliest Man in England'. The 18th century entertainer, who died on 5 September 1749 after a career of pleasing the King with his grotesque looks, was so ugly that he won a contest organized by Lord Chesterfield, who pitted him against the most revolting hag he could find in London's seedy Soho district. The artist Hogarth actually made a face-mask of him. When Heidegger saw the mock image of himself, he was so shocked that he fainted!

Maurice Tillet

The Hideous Wrestler

Maurice Tillet born in France in 1910, was a gifted, highly intelligent man who could speak 14 languages and turn his hand adroitly to virtually anything he chose. He could have had the pick of any career he wanted and, if ever the phrase applied to one man exclusively, the world really was his oyster.

Then tragedy struck. When he was in his twenties, he developed acromegaly, a rare and horrific disease which causes bones to grow wildly and uncontrollably. From an early age, it tends to turn infants into fast-growing giants. Yet at his stage in life – a life which had been so rich in promise – it turned Tillet instead into a hideously deformed parody of a human being. Within months, he had changed from a smart, reasonably handsome whizz-kid, as we would have known him today, into a grotesque distortion of a young man, frightened even to venture into public gaze.

In search of a new identity to fit his chronic disfigurement, Tillet fled to America, where he cashed in on his shattered appearance in the only way he could, by becoming a professional wrestler, billed as a fearsome, freak ogre of the ring. He was an instant success, an ironic comparison with the time when his life could have meant so much more to him. Spectators roared with delight as he – cast as a wrestling 'baddie' – grappled with other men for a living.

He resigned himself to a friendless, lonely existence, even shunning the charity of others who took pity on his misshapen form. Bones jutted into awkward positions all over his body, twisting it into what resembled a huge, anomalous mass. In the ring, he resembled some kind of nightmare contortionist as his body was so badly afflcted.

Yet Tillet himself remained a gentle giant, with the inner soul of a poet, scholar and serious man. And a few people did, somehow, manage to befriend him. One was businessman Patrick Kelly, to whose home in Braintree, Massachusetts, Tillet was often invited. Together, the two would play chess and, in rare moments of self-pity, Tillet would raise his deformed head and moan: 'How awful it is to be imprisoned in this body.'

In 1955, Tillet died. In his memory, Mr Kelly had a death mask of his tragic friend made, which he placed on his library desk. It was to mark the last of their chess games: games the two had enjoyed so much, and which had spawned a bond of friendship between a businessman and a monster.

In 1980, 25 years after Tillet's death, the games began again. This spine-chilling twist to the tale came after Mr Kelly had installed a computerized chess machine, against which he frequently played, beside the plaster cast of Tillet's head. Late one evening, the computer deviated from its programmed patterns of play and used an 18th century opening invented by a French master – a gambit the long-since dead Tillet had used consistently.

'I played out the game, and the next morning noticed that the computer was not plugged in,' says Mr Kelly. 'But I thought nothing of it at the time. Yet a few weeks later the computer used a similar opening – and again it was not connected to any power supply'. Electronic engineers made a painstaking check of the system for Mr Kelly – and discovered to their astonishment that the computer could operate without electricity as long as it was close to the death mask of the long-forgotten Tillet. Puzzled, the businessman had the plaster cast X-rayed, only to affirm the fact that it was, indeed, solid plaster.

Only one, haunting answer could remain; the ghost or, perhaps, the sensitive, gentle soul of the hideous wrestler had returned to the place and the pastime he had enjoyed the most in his tortured life – playing chess with his best friend.

Mr Kelly firmly believes this is the case, and accepts that if the unplugged computer does not work for a period of days, Tillet's spirit is absent. 'When I want a game,' he says, 'I set up the pieces without plugging the set in. If there is no response, I know that Maurice is not with me for the time being ...'

The Devil Boy

I t is difficult to imagine the depths of suffering to which a two-year-old child can sink. Yet, when he was rescued by a group of nuns in 1976, it was the first time in his tortured little life that David Lopez had ever experienced an expression of love.

His home, in a village deep in the Peruvian rain forests, was a wooden cage through whose bars pitying adults would occasionally feed him morsels of food before turning away in horror. His very survival depended on such irregular acts of charity from a native community to whom he was a living curse or 'devil boy'; a human punishment meted out to them by some hidden, potent force.

The reason behind their cruel, superstitious imprisonment of an infant was simple; baby David was born without a face. He had no mouth or upper jaw, no lips or nose. And, as time went by, it appeared that his remaining features were being relentlessly eaten away. Had he not been discovered by those travelling sisters of mercy, David Lopez – a random name with which he was later christened – would almost surely have faced a lonely, agonizing death.

Instead, he plays today with little boys his own age, goes out shopping with his adoptive mother, absorbs, bright as a button, all that he is taught and enjoys a life a world away from the nightmare he once knew. At the hands of a skilled and dedicated surgeon who is literally rebuilding his face, David has emerged from his ordeal into what is indeed a brave, new world.

The first real glimmer of hope came when a social worker at the orphanage in the Peruvian capital of Lima where David was first taken remembered seeing a televised interview in which top Scottish surgeon Ian Jackson spoke of the enormous challenge of correcting facial deformities in children.

Cutting through a mountain of red tape, the orphanage managed to organize a passport for David to travel to Britain and a visa for him to stay in the country as long as he needed. Two airline companies responded to an appeal by providing him with a free first-class flight.

Ian Jackson, whose wife Marjorie and their four children immediately agreed that David should live with them as a member of the family, offered to perform a planned series of delicate operations completely free of charge. An appeal fund organized by church officials and local newspapers, to cover the cost of National Health Service facilities for David's treatment at Cannies-burn Hospital, near Glasgow, raised more than £50,000. Despite seemingly insurmountable difficulties, in little more than a year since he was found cowering in his prison cage, David Lopez was on the verge of being re-born.

To begin with, the prospect of surgery threw up alarming complications. In an interview two years after he began work rebuilding David's face, Ian Jackson said: 'I asked myself if David knew whether he was being punished or helped because he was too young to realize what was going on. He developed chest problems, so I had to suspend surgery for quite a while.

'Some day, David may curse me for not leaving him to his fate in the jungle, but I just hope I am giving him a chance, giving him a face that will be acceptable. He will have to take it from there. David will never be considered handsome, but surgery can give him a face that will allow him to lead a normal life. He has the opportunity to develop and I think he will come out on top. He is a bright, warm and intelligent little boy.'

Initially, it was difficult to determine whether David's face had been mauled by animals or if he had been the victim of a horrendous disease. In fact, his disfigurement was the result of a rare disease called noma, a condition caused by malnutrition which usually eats away at the corners of a victim's mouth. In David's case, the disease had become rampant, relentlessly devouring his jaws, nose and upper lip. When found, he was unable to talk and responded only to a few words of Spanish, the native tongue of the South American Indians.

With the trusting, innocent love of a child, David soon accepted Ian Jackson and his wife as 'mum and dad'. A Spanish-speaking tutor was hired as he began to settle into what to him was the unknown world of the family. But there was still the problem of the tiny girl at the play school, who refused to play with 'the boy with the funny face' and holidaymakers who took their children away from the beach when David arrived to build sandcastles.

Said Ian Jackson: 'Children are straightforward and honest when confronted with people who are disfigured. They make a casual remark out of innocent curiosity, but within five minutes they have forgotten about it and accept the person. David knows he doesn't look like other children. We have explained the matter to him and now he is so accustomed to being regarded as normal that he wonders why anyone bothers to remark on his face.'

On one occasion, the surgeon continued, David was in a sweet shop, and heard the shop-keeper remark about his 'terrible face' to a customer. 'David stood behind the counter, put his thumbs up to his ears and started to waggle his fingers. He regarded it as a huge joke. To him, waggling his fingers and poking out his tongue is really pulling a terrible face. He's a tough, independent little kid. David stands up for himself and really considers himself to be a member of our family. We treat him just like we treat our own children. When he is naughty, he gets spanked, just like my own son and daughters. David accepts that as natural, and that's the way it should be. He gets his fair share of cuddling, and he appreciates the fact that we don't hide him away. When the whole family goes out shopping or on a picnic, he comes with us. We have so forgotten about David's face that sometimes it takes a moment's thought to understand why strangers are staring at him.'

David has already undergone dozens of operations in which the tips of his ribs have been cut away and transplanted inside the fragile tissue of his face to form his upper mouth and nose. And, in a series of intricate skin graft operations, tissue has been transferred to his face to cover his newly-built, man-made features. One day, that gaping hole in the middle of his face will be gone forever.

Meanwhile, his home life too is being lovingly moulded. Marjorie Jackson says: 'The family has taken David to its heart. Everyone does if they take the trouble to get to know him. When he first arrived, he couldn't, or didn't want to, communicate at all. David must have known from his earliest moments that he wasn't like other children. Before we could win his trust he had to get over whatever had happened to him in the jungle. Because of the damage to his face he couldn't attempt to speak, but we soon realized how quick and intelligent he was. We had a worrying time when he first started play school, but only one of the children reacted badly.

'He makes friends quickly among other children. It is only grown-ups who present problems. I get very angry when adults approach to tell me that I shouldn't allow him to be seen outside the house because he is so ugly. They are the ugly ones. They refuse to understand the needs of a boy like David. He can be tough and boisterous and too energetic at times. When he gets together with our son Andrew the pair of them wrestle on the floor and play rough games of football in the back garden.

'But we don't wrap him in cotton wool. All we try to do is make sure he doesn't get any bruises or cuts which will hold back the healing of his surgery.'

Surgery which is transforming the face of a dark-complexioned, piercingly dark-eyed little boy from a jungle prisoner of hate into a happy, affectionate fellow who can face the world with dignity, pride, and a fiercely independent courage born from love.

Shepherd boy genius

The son of a shepherd, Vito Mangiamele astounded experts at the French Academy of Sciences with his mathematical wizardry when they examined him on 3 July 1839. Learned scholars were speechless when Sicilian-born Vito was able to calculate the cubic root of 3,796,416 in his head in the lightning time of just 30 seconds. He was 11 at the time.

The Faceless Child

The little girl called Alice was just a few weeks old when she was rejected by her mother. The infant was considered to be too much of a burden and the poor woman made the heart-rending decision that she would never be able to cope with her or help her in later years to lead anything like a normal life. For Alice was born without a face.

She had come into the world suffering from one of nature's rarest and most cruel aberrations, a birth defect known as bilateral cleft face. Her eyelids were on the side of her head, yet she had no eyes; where her mouth should have been there were only small holes opening into soft mucous membranes; she had no nose; the very shape of her skull was distorted. She had severe problems simply breathing; she could only be fed through a tube inserted into her neck. It seemed that whatever future the stricken baby might have would be a nightmarish one in a sightless, shuttered world as far removed from an ordinary life as it might be possible to imagine.

Alice's first good fortune came when a nurse, Thelma Perkins, at the University of Tennessee Hospital in Knoxville where she was born, fell in love with the tragic infant and, with her husband Raymond, became her legal guardian. Thelma said: 'Alice was only one hour old when I first saw her . . . and I cried that any little baby should be born like that.'

Astonishingly, apart from the appearance of her face, her breathing problems and the difficulties attached to feeding her, Alice was healthy. Today, at the time of writing, she is 6 years old – and beginning to reap the benefits of her second stroke of luck which is, against all the odds, helping her learn to lead a life which, though it may never be perfectly normal, is far removed from the tortured existence it seemed she had been destined to lead.

Dr John Lynch, a plastic surgeon at the Vanderbilt Hospital saw her plight and is now, in a series of remarkable operations, rebuilding her face. He is pioneering advances in what he says is only the seventh documented case of bilateral cleft face in medical history. But it is a slow, delicate and nerve-racking process, fraught with uncertainty and the natural impatience of Thelma and Raymond Perkins, who are awaiting official clearance to adopt Alice as their own child, to see her progress.

Alice has undergone 11 painstaking operations so far and now has gums, teeth – which could not previously grow inside her disfigured mouth – and a nose which has an artificial bone taken from one of her ribs. Because no grafted-on nose could grow with the rest of her, Dr Lynch has given her an adult-sized one. Her mouth has been totally reconstructed, and Alice, having quickly learned how to move her tongue and jaws, has begun to eat semi-solid food; the tube attached to her oesophagus having at last, mercifully, been rendered useless.

Dr Lynch has also strengthened and completely reshaped Alice's skull and moved her eyelids to the correct positions on her rapidly changing face. The surgeon estimates that he will be required to perform a whole string of operations until she is 18 years old, by which time, he believes, Alice will be able to step out into a brave new world, with a completely new – and, he says, perfectly normal – face.

The total cost of the surgery will be about 300,000 dollars. The state of Tennessee has already contributed in excess of 60,000 dollars and the United Brotherhood of Carpenters and Joiners, of which Raymond Perkins is a member, has raised 23,000 dollars from members across the country. Fund-raising efforts are continuing, and thanks to the overwhelming generosity of public bodies and private citizens, Alice seems certain of her previously unthinkable bright prospects for the future.

For the time being, though, she is progressing by leaps and bounds. Although she is, of course, blind and still has a few problems with her mouth, she is learning at a fantastic rate. She can talk, following continued help from speech therapists and has been enrolled in a special education class. 'She has even learned to sing a little bit,' says her proud foster mother.

The use of skilled plastic surgery to correct and improve hideous facial deformities may sound like 20th century 'miracle medicine', yet such surgery, although obviously nowhere near as sophisticated, was being performed almost a century ago. The *International Medical Magazine* of Philadelphia reported a case in its issue of February 1894, in which a 72-year-old man with an enormous, disfiguring facial growth with an estimated weight of two pounds was rid of his deformity by plastic surgery.

In 1892, Dr J. P. Parker of Kansas City restored the missing bridge of a patient's nose by transplanting the bone and tissue of the second joint of his little finger in a then quite unique 'plastic operation'. Yet such surgery in those days was a rarity and for generations, tragic characters such as the Elephant Man were forced to live with their dreadful deformities. It is only relatively recent development that has enabled such savagely afflicted victims such as David Lopez and little Alice to look to the future with hope.

By a neck

It is well known that certain native tribes indulge in the practice of stretching their necks to giraffe-like proportions by using tightly-fitting copper coils to encourage unnatural growth. But it is quite astonishing to recount that the maximum extension recorded is one of 15¾ inches, achieved by a member of the Karen or Padaung tribe of Burma.

Chapter Two

Freaks of Mind and Memory

Freak Senses

It is often said that if one human faculty is impaired, the body compensates by sharpening the rest of the senses. In the 19th century, after she was struck deaf, dumb and blind, a girl called Helen Keller became the world's most baffling medical oddity, because she could distinguish colours simply by touching them and people simply by sniffing them.

She was examined by doctors and public audiences, who marvelled not only at her incredibly developed freak senses but also her remarkable courage. She became famous across America as 'the girl with eyeless sight', and, in a tremendous victory over her own infirmities, managed to succeed in gaining several university degrees.

Helen Keller had been a perfectly normal, happy little girl at her family home in Alabama until tragedy struck when she was 19 months old. She contracted a virulent fever which gave her delirium, convulsions and a raging temperature which doctors were convinced would kill her. After three days, however, it became apparent that she *would* survive against all the odds – although joy quickly turned to heartbreak again when her parents were told that the ravages of the fever would leave their bright-as-a-button little girl permanently deaf, dumb and blind.

Until she reached the age of 8, Helen's mother and father nursed and cared for her as best they could – though it soon became obvious that they were unable to educate or even discipline her; she had developed into a physically strong girl given, occasionally, to violent temper tantrums. Their situation was desperate; their sense of love and loyalty made them reluctant to send Helen to a home where she would have been cared for but, more than likely, would never have progressed.

It was at that stage that a Miss Sullivan from the Perkins Institute for the Blind in South Boston became interested in Helen, and determined to try to teach her to manage simple day-to-day tasks and how to behave. It soon became apparent to Miss Sullivan that Helen had a bright and agile mind and, with the help of another teacher, Sarah Fuller, Helen began to absorb a little and then a lot of information about the world in which she had previously been a total stranger.

Miss Fuller, an expert in speech therapy for the deaf, began by teaching Helen the manual alphabet – spelling out letters and words on the palm of her hand. Slowly, the silent and incomprehensible darkness which had enveloped the tragic little girl began to fade away. Helen began to learn more and more

Helen Keller

quickly, until she was able, using the hand signals she had mastered, to tell Miss Fuller what she wanted to do next. She wanted to learn how to speak. Miss Fuller was delighted.

Despite the disapproval of Helen's parents, Miss Fuller began the lessons which would eventually lead the little girl into a life where she would constantly be in the public eye; where crowds would gaze in awe and admiration at a curiosity whose achievements almost defied belief.

Helen's first lesson lasted two hours and involved tracing her fingers, tentatively at first, around the outline of Miss Fuller's face, mouth and neck. She discovered every part of her patient teacher's mouth, tongue, teeth, lips and palate until she understood how vital they all were for the power of speech. Miss Fuller then began to shape Helen's own mouth for making basic vowel sounds and placed the eager child's hand on her windpipe so that she could feel the vibrations. Next, she placed Helen's fingers on her tongue, so that she could feel the movement it made when she uttered a noise. The teacher was astounded when Helen's hands flew to her own mouth and throat and repeated the sound she had just made so perfectly that it could have been an echo.

Six years after making that first sound, Helen Keller could speak. Despite the fact that she still could not see or hear, her remaining senses, unaccountably, became so finely attuned that she actually learned to 'feel' colours. The only way she could explain this incredible freak phenomenon was by saying that to her sensitive fingers, different colours seemed to radiate different forms of energy which she was capable of picking up. Later, this remarkable eyeless sight enabled her to appreciate the rich colours of an oil painting; she could 'see' with her fingertips the magnificent hues of a sunset on canvas just as others could see them with their eyes.

Helen also developed an acute, unerringly accurate sense of smell; where normal people so easily distinguished friends and relatives simply by looking at them, Helen could detect them with her nose. When upset, she would run to her mother simply by following the scent! Throughout her life, she could uncannily sense which of her friends or colleagues were in the room with her before they made themselves known by using the manual alphabet.

Her nimble mind helped her earn several university degrees and in her twenties Helen became the talk of America, with a series of tours, public meetings and lectures which she gave in the hope of helping others like herself. Hands, nose, speech and intuition turned her into a celebrity – and a sensation in the medical world. With true dignity though, she never joined the garish and crude peep show circuit, preferring to tour independently and use her special gifts to try to open up a new world for others in darkness and despair.

Eyeless Sight

The miraculous freak phenomenon of eyeless sight – despite the incredible levels of awareness to which Helen Keller took it – is, in fact, centuries old. British scientist Robert Boyle reported the case of a 17th century man, John Vermaasen, who was totally blind in both eyes but could, nevertheless, distinguish colours. Using ribbons placed between his fingers, Vermaasen accurately identified every colour, explaining that black had the same feel as very coarse sand or the points of needles, whereas red felt as smooth as silk. Strangely, this freak sense was particularly acute in Vermaasen's thumbs and seemed to be heightened when he had been fasting.

Kuda Bux was a quiet, unassuming Kashmiri man who, although not blind, supplied powerful persuasion to the medical world that eyeless sight – or extra-retinal vision as it has since become known – is a freak sense possessed by certain people.

Skilled in the art of Yoga after years of intensive study of the mental powers required to use it, Bux gave stage performances of eyeless sight all over the world during the 1930s. He vowed that his ability to distinguish colour and perform skilled feats while totally blindfolded was genuine, and in 1934 his claims were put to the test by a panel of medical experts and scientists. They blindfolded him by putting lumps of dough on his eyes and then wrapping them in metal foil and several layers of gauze and woollen bandage. When they were finally satisfied that there was no possible way that he could use his eyesight, they placed books in front of him, from which they asked him to read. Bux then astounded the panel by giving a faultless performance.

A similar investigation into his powers was carried out in Montreal, Canada, in 1938. The result was the same – flawless. Further proof of his ability to use extra-retinal vision came in September, 1937 in Liverpool when, balanced on a narrow ledge, blindfolded as before and 200 feet above the ground, he walked the entire length of the roof on his precarious perch with ease. Touring in America in 1945, he astonished onlookers by again demonstrating his powers by riding a bicycle blindfolded through the busy traffic of New York's Times Square.

Another remarkable eyeless sight case is that of Laura Dewey Bridgman, born on 21 December, 1829, who was left deaf and totally blind in her right eye, with only very slight vision in her left, at the age of 2 after contracting scarlet fever. Like Helen Keller, Laura was exceptionally bright, and quickly surpassed all her classmates at the Massachusetts Asylum for the Blind.

Her finely developed sense of touch included a peculiar sensitivity to vibration – and she could even 'hear' music with her fingertips. Her musical digits enabled her to tell the difference between a full and a half note, a feat which many people who can hear are incapable of doing. She even developed her sense of touch through her feet. She was able to detect the comings and goings of people by picking up vibrations in the ground.

The astonishing case of a totally blind Brooklyn woman, Mollie Fancher, who claimed to have an eyeless sight sense in the top of her head, was reported in 1893. Doctors were completely baffled by the way she could read an ordinary book – in light or darkness – simply by running her fingertips across the printed page.

The Unseen Hand

One of the world's most amazing living mental freaks is a young man from Linton, near Cambridge, England. Matthew Manning was just 16 when, he claims, he met a 300-year-old ghost at his home in 1971. Over the next few years, he says, he conversed with the figure, who called himself Robert Webbe, and made drawings of him – a hunched character in 17th century dress who walked with two sticks.

Later, Matthew found that he had the power of 'automatic writing', when another mind acted as an unseen hand to guide his own hand and his pen. Names, dates and details of local history passed on in this way tallied completely with facts buried away in archives. And, through contacting Webbe, the boy discovered that he had bizarre paranormal powers. He could bend cutlery with his mind, stop watches and prevent electricity flowing, in much the same way as that achieved by so-called 'super-static' people.

For a few years, Matthew toured the world giving demonstrations and exhibitions of his powers, but he soon tired of entertaining, complaining that he felt like a performing monkey. He turned to psychic healing, lecturing and healing through Europe and Australasia. And, in America, he proved that he had the ability to affect blood and cancer cells, even in sealed test tubes.

He still continues to use his mysterious but beneficial powers, as an inspiring example of the uses to which freak senses can be put.

Teeth

It is quite common for infants to be born with teeth, but perhaps the most distinguished example is that of Prince Louis Dieudonné, later Louis XIV of France, who arrived in the world with two milk teeth on 5 September 1683. Another curiosity is the case published in 1896 of a Frenchman who late in life grew his *fourth* (and final) set of teeth.

The Human Mole

'**O**rdinary attractions ... no longer hold excitement for crowds. They want to see something sensational and macabre – and Norman Green fits the bill. He's the most spectacular freak on Earth.'

Those words, which could easily have been purloined from the peepshow patter of Phineas T. Barnum a century or so ago, were, in fact, spoken by showbusiness agent Bernard Wooly on Saturday 17 July, 1982; the eve of a summer fun-fair in Preston, Lancashire. With a wily eye for the outrageous, Mr Wooly was drumming-up customers who, for 25 pence a go, could see his latest star sitting on a settee. It was perfect timing on Mr Wooly's part; for people all over the country had only that day been reading about Norman Green, the Human Mole.

Father-of-six Norman hit instant freak appeal the day after he nervously abandoned his home of eight years – a 21-inch deep dugout under the floorboards of the house in Wigan where, with the exception of his wife Pauline, his family lived in total ignorance of his underground existence. As he clambered, blinking into the daylight, a tangled Rip Van Winkle beard and matted grey hair hanging two feet down his back completed his remarkable, mole-like appearance. He had re-emerged from that tiny hole after, quite simply, vanishing from the world eight years previously.

Norman, 43, a former travelling salesman, literally went to ground shortly before Christmas 1974, after being questioned by police about a serious offence. (When he finally re-appeared, it was decided that no charges would be made against him). Aided by his wife, who was to explain to friends and neighbours that he had deserted her and the children, Norman decided that his only course of action was to 'hole-up' indefinitely in the coffin-sized space under the floorboards of the family lounge. A settee was placed over the hiding-place so there would be no clues that he was there.

By night, Norman would be given food and drink by his wife and, occasionally, emerge from the foundations of the semi-detached council house. But by day he remained silently entombed. Pauline Green later said: 'It was terrible when friends and relatives came to call. I would be chatting and laughing with them, and all the time I knew they were sitting on top of Norman.

'I had to remove all trace of Norman. I even had to give his clothes away so people would really believe he had gone. He only ever emerged at night or, sometimes, when the house was empty, and he had to wear my clothes whenever he came out. One of the saddest moments was when one of my sons said to me: "My dad is going to come back one of these days with a lot of money and a fast car". I hated living a lie. To the outside world I was a divorcee. But every time I went back to the house I knew I was going back to the world of deceit. The pressure just got too much to bear. I just wanted to be like every other wife and mother. I wanted to go out at nights with my husband. I wanted to go to the park with him and the kids. I was envious of other wives – and I only went through it all because I love Norman so much. It was for his sake.'

Shopping expeditions became an ordeal for Pauline, who carefully ensured that she did not buy too much to arouse suspicions. Sympathetic neighbours, who believed she really had been abandonded by Norman, even rallied round to give her hand-me-down clothes and cash. As time wore on, Norman became a distant memory, and no-one in their wildest dreams could have begun to guess that he was alive and well and actually underfoot whenever anyone visited the family home. Indeed, it seemed that Norman had so perfectly slipped away into his Human Mole role that he would never be discovered.

What Norman had not counted on, however, was the childlike curiosity of little Kristian Coates, a three-year-old boy from across the road. While he should have been playing with his pals, Kristian cheekily wandered through an open front door and into the lounge of the Green family home. There, the astonished youngster watched in horror as the red-flowered carpet seemed to move by itself. Then, the furniture began to move and the floorboards under the settee began to creak and groan eerily. Suddenly, the floorboards were flung open and a gaunt, hairy figure began to emerge from the darkened hollow below. Norman must have been as shocked as little Kristian, who fled tearfully from his creepy encounter with the Human Mole. For it was the first mistake he had made since burying himself away from the world.

For three more years though, his subterranean sanctuary remained undiscovered, because nobody would take seriously what they believed was the wild fantasy of a little boy who kept repeating: 'I went into the room and saw the furniture moving. Then I saw this strange man come out from under the floorboards. He had long hair and a beard. He was horrible.'

Kristian's parents finally did decide to keep an eye on the house over the road when, as his father said: 'I began to notice little things that suggested Norman was still there. Pauline would go to the shops and buy cigarettes, but she didn't smoke. She would also buy beer from the off-licence and she went to the betting shop clutching wads of betting slips. (Incredibly, Norman managed to maintain his interest in horse racing, following form in the newspapers his wife would occasionally give him). I used to lie awake wondering whether I should tell the police. But how could I? It was such an incredible story.'

Eventually, Kristian's mother rather uncertainly did relay their growing belief that Norman might, somehow, still be around to the police. And, three days later, a couple of local bobbies came knocking on the Greens' door, and before long Norman the Human Mole was surfacing again after an almost unbelievable eight years. Norman, and possibly to a lesser extent, his wife and family, now had to face astounded friends and neighbours.

Soon, as newspapers and offers to appear as a freak show attraction began to land on his doorstep, all he could find to say to an incredulous world was: 'I almost got to like it down there. I'm sure I could go back quickly to living the way I did for eight years. In fact, there has been so much fuss I sometimes wish I had never come out.'

Engraving of a pig-faced lady.

Sisters of Mystery

Twins Greta and Freda Chaplin are Britain's sisters of mystery. A quirk of nature has created them totally identical in mind, body, behaviour and even emotion. They are absolute mirror images of one another; living so perfectly in unison that they sometimes conjure up the idea that they might have been cloned in the style of only the wildest of science fiction fantasies.

They have been called 'The Terrible Twins', 'The Pests', and various other names in a blaze of newspaper publicity which has driven them into deep retreat from prying eyes. And, as though they were singing a duet, they say together with impeccable timing: 'We want to get away from people staring at us, laughing at us ... the unkindness.'

It is true that their bizarre, unrequited love-in-tandem for a Yorkshire lorry driver landed them in a courtroom and at the centre of controversy. But, equally, they have become victims too; time-warped back to the days of the Victorian peep show by a new public lust for the true freak.

Greta and Freda, 39, spent six weeks in jail between May and June 1981. They were sentenced after a series of court warnings to stop their 20-year pursuit and harassment of 56-year-old near neighbour Ken Iveson, the unwilling object of their dual passion. Medical experts called to give evidence admitted that they were completely baffled by the twins' exact physical and mental make-up, let alone their illegal duplicity. The judge who sentenced them released them two weeks early 'as an exercise purely of mercy.'

Lorry driver Iveson, who lived near the twins in Moore Avenue, York for many years, later explained: 'Wherever one went, the other was walking behind. They never played with the other kids in the street when they were young. My trouble with them began when I ticked them off for throwing torn newspapers into my parents' garden. After that, they were always hanging about me and pulling faces at me. Their obsession grew and grew. They followed me everywhere, popping up from behind walls.'

Into adulthood, the infatuation followed, until a mighty legal hand fell at the same time upon the shoulders of Greta and Freda. Now they live together in a hostel in York, maintaining their remarkable double act.

They have always worn the same clothes, even to the extent as schoolgirls of swopping a sock each if their mother sent them out in different coloured pairs. And, uncannily, they burst into tears at the same time at the slightest hint that they might ever be separated. They sob: 'Nothing will ever make us hate each other. We will always do everything together.'

On the twins' release from prison, a social worker gave them each a bar of soap as a present. The bars were different colours, so they cut each in two and swopped halves. Their eating habits are identical. They have been seen to put food in their mouths simultaneously and finish their meals at precisely the same time. Their powers of telepathy, explored to the limit of current understanding, remain as mysterious as their facsimile lifestyle. Sometimes they speak in unison. Sometimes one begins a sentence and the other finishes it.

Dr Wilfred Hume, of Leeds University Department of Psychiatry, who has studied Greta and Freda at length, has said: 'I have never come across anything like this case. They are very dependent on each other. And now they have got to this stage in their lives it is unlikely they will change. The only problem is going to come when one of them dies. The remaining one would either cope, eventually, after a period of stress, or, perhaps more likely, die very shortly afterwards.'

Following their release from jail, Greta and Freda reported to a local hospital every day for occupational therapy. Their efforts would include flower arranging or handicrafts, and very often their work was identical.

The twins still do their shopping together; carrying their identical purchases home in identical plastic bags, from the same local supermarket. According to their social worker at the hostel: 'They are free to walk away from here whenever they choose. But they don't want to go. They do absolutely everything together. I have never seen them apart.'

In a frank interview with the London *Daily Star*, Greta and Freda have spoken of the strange mental bond that ties them together like inseparable Siamese twins. At school, they say, they always insisted on sitting together, and would scream if any teacher tried to separate them. And, speaking virtually always in unison, they add: 'We have always been like this, all our lives. Speaking together just comes naturally to us. We do everything together; dress the same, have a bath together and we like the same kind of food. We go everywhere together. We are never apart.'

Sadly, and almost like fairytale caricatures of themselves, they explain public reaction to them: 'People are always looking at us, laughing in the street. But they hadn't better say anything. No they hadn't better. No they hadn't better. People have been hurtful and unkind to us. We want to find a place of our own to live together. We must be together. Nothing interests us much. We are only happy together.'

Dr David Westbury, of Winterburn Hospital, Tees-side, who has also studied the twins in depth, says: 'There is certainly no medical explanation or medical solution. All that can be done . . . has been done.' Which means that Greta and Freda Chaplin must remain, together, sisters of mystery.

Greta and Freda Chaplin

Amazing Memories

The machinations of the mind all add up to a mystery for most of us. And usually, the sum total of our mental arithmetic amounts to a struggle to tot up the addition of a restaurant bill. But for some people, being a mastermind is simply child's play.

Little Oscar Moore first demonstrated his powers when he was just 3 years old. Born to poor parents at Waco, Texas on 19 August 1885, Oscar became the sole attraction of the city's Central Music Hall, where the awesome assembly of brainpower focused its attention on his remarkable skills.

The toddler was not only super-intelligent, but he could also soak up information so swiftly that his mind had become an encyclopaedic marvel before he was even able to walk. It is rare to find a case of total memory recall coupled with genius. It was even rarer in Oscar's case, for he was blind.

A likeable, affectionate little boy, Oscar quickly won the hearts and minds of his intellectual mentors, establishing an easy rapport with men who despite years of study and devotion often struggled to keep pace with his darting, probing brain. Way before his teens, he was to become not simply university material but a rival in genius to the most learned men of any country. Exactly what freak of nature caused his incredible mental prowess remains a mystery, but it is an aberration which has been repeated on a number of occasions throughout the centuries.

Eight years before Oscar was bewildering the best scholars America had to offer, an 11-year-old boy was found wandering the streets of Marseilles in France with a trick monkey on his back, a begging bowl in his hand and a neat line in patter. There was, however, more to unkempt little Jacques Inaudi that met the eye. One of his favourite money raising ruses was to bet strangers that he could solve any mental problem they cared to set him. It never failed, for behind the beggar-boy façade, Jacques was capable of what today would be computer-speed reaction in answering mathematical mind-benders.

Memory man

The world's most incredible 'Memory Man' is Mehmed Ali Halici of Ankara, Turkey who, on 14 October 1967, recited an astonishing 6,666 verses of the Koran by memory in six hours. Mehmed's perfect recall was monitored by half a dozen leading academics who verified his claim to a world record.

Giant emperor

Emperor Maximus of Rome was an amazing man mountain. He was a giant, reputedly towering well over eight feet, with huge overgrown features believed to have been caused by the rare disorder known as acromegaly, which can result in great physical strength. Indeed Maximus, a former shepherd, delighted in taking on heavyweight wrestlers two at a time. His sense of fun was not shared by his own soldiers, who killed him as he slept on 17 June AD 238.

Mini-mastermind

A little Korean boy called Kim became the mini-mastermind of the world after he was born on 7 March 1963, to parents who were both university professors born on the same day in the same year at exactly the same time. Baby superbrain Kim understood integral calculus at the age of four and mastered four languages before starting school. His IQ has been calculated at 210. It was not previously thought possible to exceed 200.

Jacques' rare talent quickly drew the attention of a well-to-do resident of Marseilles who, astonished by the boy's intelligence, took him to Paris for examination by the city's famous Anthropological Society in 1880.

There, he confounded the leading lights of the academic world by solving in less than ten minutes in his head a multiplication of numbers running into trillions by numbers running into billions. When asked exactly what process he had used to arrive at the correct answer, it was discovered that he worked backwards in his head from left to right instead of the usual right to left method which most people use either in their heads or on paper. Under the wing of scholastic luminaries the future for little Jacques, the former street urchin, was secure. But, in his thirst for knowledge, his first request was not for weighty mathematical tomes or a set of problem equations; he asked if he could first learn to read and write!

One of the leading adult mental arithmetic freaks of the era was America Rube Fields, from Johnson County, Missouri, who was described as a 'shiftless, idle fellow' who during his childhood had refused to go to school on the grounds that education would turn him into 'as big a fool as other people.' In his forties when first pounced on by academics keen to unlock the secret of his mental abilities, Fields is said have been able to answer any mathematical problem in less time that it took to ask it. One report at the time said: 'Give Rube Fields the distance by rail between any two points, and the dimensions of a car wheel, and almost as soon as the statement has left your lips he will tell you the number of revolutions the wheel will make in travelling over the track. Call four or five or any number of columns of figures down a page, and when you have reached the bottom he will announce the sum.' His answers were quick and sharp, seemingly by intuition. Fields himself could not give any explanation for his uncanny power. Despite offers, Fields steadfastly refused to go on public exhibit for circus or peep show bosses anxious to acquire his talents, although he did earn occasional money from attending scientific conferences and the like.

Modern day memory masters include Dutch born Willem Klein, who holds the world record for the fastest extraction of a 13th root from a 100 digit number in 1 minute 28.8 seconds at the National Laboratory for High Energy Physics in Tsukuba, Japan, on 7 April 1981.

Indian-born Mrs Shakuntala Devi lived up to her name of the 'Human Computer' when she came up with the answer of a multiplication of two 13-digit numbers chosen at random by the Computer Department of Imperial College, London, in an astonishing 28 seconds on 18 June 1980. The size of the problem can perhaps best be gauged by her correct answer: 18,947,668,177,995,426,462,773,730.

On the world's accepted indeces for intelligence quotients 150 represents genius level. Only one person in 10,000 has an I.Q. above 160. In terms of national averages, Japan leads the world with 106.6. The British national average is around 100.

From brain power to the brain itself (though it doesn't naturally follow that big-heads are egg-heads!) Largest brained characters in history include Oliver Cromwell and Lord Byron, though the heaviest verified weight of a human brain was that of a 50 year old male which was gauged at 4 pounds 8.29 ounces by Dr Thomas F. Hegert, Chief Medical Examiner for District 9 of the State of Florida on 23 October 1975. The smallest brain ever recorded was that of writer Anatole France (1844-1924) which barely tipped the scales at only 4.126 ounces.

Chapter
Three

Men or Monsters?

The Monster Makers

Bertholde, a terribly deformed dwarf, rose from the lowly rank of court jester to become prime minister of the sixth century kingdom of Lombardy; from comic freak to feared politician. Little is know of the origin of this strange, stunted figure, other than that he was almost certainly a monster made and not a monster born.

Bertholde, it is widely believed, was a human product of a secret and sinister organization which procured slave children and then, using sickening techniques, turned its terrified little captives into hideously deformed freaks. In his famous novel *The Man Who Laughs*, Victor Hugo describes the organization as *Comprachicos* (the child-buyers) and says: 'They worked on human beings as the Chinese work on trees ... they could mark a child as though he were a pocket handkerchief ... they produced toys for men.'

In a work published in 1619, Dr Carlos Garcia refers to later sects of monster makers as the Dacianos, and says: 'They kidnap children three or four years old and, breaking their arms and legs, lame and disfigure them so that they may afterwards sell them to beggars, blind men and other vagabonds.'

Throughout history, the demand for human freaks has exceeded supply and created a nightmarish series of enterprises aimed at satisfying the public thirst for the bizarre.

The following extract is perhaps the most chilling of Hugo's accounts of the monster makers:

'In order that a human toy should prove a success, he must be taken in hand early. The dwarf must be fashioned when young ... a well-formed child is not very amusing; a hunchback is better fun. Hence grew an art. There were trainers who took a man and made him an abortion; they took a face and made a muzzle; they stunted growth; they distorted the features. The artificial production of teratological cases had its rules. It was quite a science; what one can imagine as the opposite of orthopedy ...'

Teratology, the science or study of monstrosities, abnormalities or malformations in animals, plants and humans, captivated the world long before the word itself crept into the language.

In ancient Egypt, the demand for dwarfs as court jesters was so great that the Cairo National Museum today boasts an astonishing collection of hundreds of figurines of these miniature monsters. Writer and archaeologist George Ebers describes how they were created, either by bringing up a child in a box which would cramp and distort its body, or by strapping it onto a

Bertholde

Gluttony

One of the most extreme and extraordinary cases of gluttony was that of a 19th century Parisian zoo-keeper, who, apart from keeping a prize collection of the dung of every animal in his care, distinguished himself also by completely devouring, over the course of only a few days, the entire carcass of a lion which had been slaughtered. He eventually, but certainly not surprisingly, died of indigestion after chomping his way through a meal of 8 pounds of hot bread.

---

board with its limbs contorted into weird positions until the bones became fixed out of joint.

In ancient Rome, there was a special market, the *Forum Morionum*, where only freaks were sold. Plutarch reported that people passed over beautiful slave girls and boys to buy deformities. Noble and wealthy ladies assembled huge troupes of freaks, especially midgets and dwarfs, for a hobby in the same way rich women today might build up large collections of jewellery or fine furs.

These human toys or work-pets were virtually all products of monster-makers whose techniques may well have been passed on from the Orient. Centuries earlier, the Chinese had learned that by binding it tightly from birth, a tiny foot could be produced. Quickly, they learned that by binding heads, legs, arms or indeed any part of the body, a child would develop lifelong deformities.

Indeed, the unbelievably cruel and inhuman monster-making process continued till comparatively recent times. On 15 May 1878, the *China Mail* newspaper reported:

'Young children are bought or stolen at a tender age and placed in a *ch'ing*, or vase with a narrow neck, and having in this case a movable bottom. In this receptacle the unfortunate little wretches are kept for years in a sitting posture, their heads outside being all the while carefully tended and fed ... When the child has reached the age of twenty or over, he or she is taken away to some distant place and "discovered" in the woods as a wild man or woman.'

The ancient Romans also experimented in producing dwarfs from stunted children by dietary deprivation, withholding lime-salts, the lack of which was thought to produce rickets. More crudely, the joints of youngsters intended to become tumblers or contortionists were skilfully dislocated at an early age. After the fall of Rome, however, it appears that the art of monster-making, as well as the general interest in freaks, became lost to Europe for more than a thousand years.

In 1400, as Tamerlane swept through India at the head of his fearsome Mongolian army, fleeing Hindustani tribes, who became the ancestors of modern gipsies, migrated westwards. Among their tribes was a caste of people skilled in the manufacture of freaks. This caste, later to become known as the Dacianos, to which Dr Garcia referred two centuries on, had its base in Spain but also members in England, who apparently used to meet in an old square tower in what is now the county of Cleveland. In Europe, the evil Dacianos supplied disfigured human fodder to feed an appetite for possessing freaks which was equally as voracious as that of the Romans ten centuries before.

An English doctor, who practised in China during the 1880s, described seeing 'animal-children' whose appearance he believed was the work of skilled and highly technical surgery. He claimed that dealers kidnapped small children and, literally, skinned them alive, bit by bit, replacing human flesh with pieces of hide cut from living dogs or bear cubs. The grafting, which modern medical experts say would be impossible to perform successfully, apparently took months. Then, the poor child's vocal chords were severed and its arm and leg joints cruelly dislocated so that is was forced to run on all fours.

Such brutal infliction of pain was not unheard of in England, where the most popular type of freak for decades was the 'Human Cock' who crowed each hour of the night. To produce a man-rooster, an operation was performed on his larynx when he was still a child so he could make no other sound than a strange, throaty crow. It is claimed that 'Human Cocks' even became traditional, or even obligatory, at court where they appeared at the whim of kings.

By the 19th century, it seems, the mysterious society of the Dacianos had vanished without trace. Its legacy, in England at least, was a keen, morbid fascination with the human freak. This gradually developed into an obsession which spawned the Victorian peep show and, across the ocean in a young America, the money-spinning showmanship of Phineas T. Barnum. The monster makers had well and truly left their mark.

Human fly

American George Willig became the world's greatest human fly on 26 May 1977, when he achieved the highest ever climb up the vertical face of a building, scaling the 1,350 foot World Trade Centre in New York in 3½ hours at a rate of 6.4 feet per minute.

The hunchback of Memphis

In January 1982, a strange, appallingly bowed intruder snatched a teenage girl from the home of her wealthy parents – and, in a macabre re-enactment of the story of Quasimodo, the Hunchback of Notre Dame, took her to live with him in a filthy, secluded church attic.

After Leslie Marie Gattas, aged 15, was finally set free by her hideously stooping captor, police in America launched one of their most incredible manhunts ever, for the 'Hunchback of Memphis'. They have named their suspect, who is still at liberty, as a man called Ernest Earle Stubblefield, a 270-pound giant whose back is permanently bent by a terrible disfigurement.

Allegedly, the lonely, tormented hunchback treated young Leslie as an adopted, though trapped, daughter throughout her terrifying ordeal. By day, they slept in a tiny crawl space in the attic. By night, the hunchback would take his treasured victim down into the church itself, or even outside for walks. Memphis cops later revealed that they played gackgammon, watched a television which the hunchback had installed in the attic and lived on food stolen from the church refrigerator.

Says Leslie: 'He was a very lonely man. He treated me well, but all the time he knew that my only thoughts were on how I could escape. He didn't touch me or harm me physically in any way. In a sense I feel great pity for him, because his mind must be incredibly mixed-up. He has the appearance of a monster, yet although what he did to me was terrible, I am not sure that he is the evil ogre the world now thinks he is.'

Carolyn Browder, a close friend of the Gattas family told an American newspaper of the bizarre night that the twisted hunchback climbed through a house window and got into the bedroom where Leslie lay sleeping.

He tied her up and drove her through Memphis to the Christ United Church in the Gattas family car, which he had stolen. It was 12 hours before Leslie's family called the police, thinking that she had simply wandered off with a girl friend who was also missing from her home at the time.

During her four-month kidnap ordeal, Leslie tried desperately to summon rescue by dropping concealed notes around the church whenever she was taken out for moonlight walks by her hunchback captor. But, ironically, the church pastor, Reverend Gerry Corlew, dismissed the scribbled pleas for help as the work of cranks. At one stage, police actually searched the attic, as they turned the city of Memphis upside down in their hunt, but they failed to look in the camouflaged crawl space where Leslie and the hunchback lay hidden.

Leslie was finally rescued in April by two maintenance men who were armed with an axe-handle and a table leg, hoping to catch vandals or youngsters trying to steal church possessions. They spotted Leslie and her hunchback tormentor on one of their bizarre midnight prowls. One of the men, 55-year-old Milton Bennett, recalls: 'We couldn't believe our eyes. But we knew instantly that it was Leslie being held by the hunchback because there had been so many pictures of her in the local newspapers while the police search was being carried out.

'My partner and I immediately went for the hunchback. I managed to get him with one blow on the back of his neck with the table leg I was carrying. He was just like a wild animal. He never said a word. But he was hurt, and when he saw that we were prepared to use our weapons again, he just backed off and fled. He was so fast, we didn't stand a chance of catching him.'

Leslie later identified the 42-year-old Stubblefield as her strange, almost pathetic kidnapper from police 'mug shot' photo-files. Fingerprints taken from the church matched up – and the search is still going on for the now-identified 'Hunchback of Memphis', whose ex-wife, Ann Clarke, of Haleyville, Alabama, says: 'He has always been obsessed with violence and religion, possibly as some kind of unaccountable result of his deformity. He had wanted to take our daughter Patti, who is 17, to live with him in Memphis, but I would not allow it. When I heard of the kidnapping I realized that in his twisted mind Leslie had become a kind of surrogate replacement for her.'

Hunchbacks are a much rarer sight nowadays than they once were, mainly because most cases are not so severe that the bone disorder cannot be treated.

One of the most incredible stories concerning these figures, now immortalized by Hollywood horror films, unfolded on 13 July 1842 when 60 hapless hunchbacks were thrown into jail in London as police scoured the city for the misshapen wretch who had attempted to shoot Queen Victoria as she rode in her carriage with King Leopold of Belgium. The innocent freaks were eventually freed when hunchback John William Bean was arrrested and sentenced to 18 months in jail – a light sentence because his gun had only been loaded with pieces of clay pipe.

Hunchback dwarf

How many scholars realize that the great essayist Alexander Pope suffered the ignominy – as, indeed, he is known to have thought it was – of being a freak twice over? He was, in fact, both dwarf and hunchback, standing barely four feet tall and with an atrociously bowed, stooping body. Of his appalling afflictions, however, he is never known to have complained.

The Limbless Wonder

An elderly nurse gently cradled the newborn infant in her arms and quietly wept as she whispered: 'Ah, the poor little thing. God will take him and it will be all for the best.' It was the first prophecy in the life of Arthur MacMurrough Kavanagh.

He was born, on 25 March 1831, into the ancestral home of Boris, County Carlow, amid vast estates in Southern Ireland whose owners through eight centuries had helped shape the country's history. His mother was Lady Harriet Margaret Le Poer Trench, second wife of Thomas Kavanagh, MP, a descendant of the Kings of Leinster. Yet, though high society had been eagerly awaiting the infant's arrival, there was no rejoicing when Arthur came into the world. No dreams or hopes for a baby boy whose life of pomp and privilege would be beyond question. Only the heart-rending words of the family nurse.

Fortunately, however, her prophecy proved wrong. Arthur lived 58 years, becoming one of the most famous characters in an already glittering dynasty, proving himself an accomplished sportsman, horseman and hunter and, eventually, an adroit and respected politician. Indeed, he was one of the most remarkable characters of the 19th century, which was truly amazing, for he was born without limbs.

Where his arms should have been, there were only two little stumps a few inches long. There were no legs at all. But such were Arthur's achievements, that it was said there was only one sad thing about him; his deep blue eyes. And such was his fighting spirit, that he never once displayed an inferiority complex.

He taught himself to write 'in a good hand' by gripping a pen between his teeth. He developed a keen intellect, shining as a youth in academic studies. But from an early age, he derived his greatest joy from his skill as one of the most able horsemen in Ireland, rarely missing a local hunt meeting. By leaning his broad shoulders forward, he could grip the reins with his two arm stumps, while strapped onto the horse in a specially-made chair saddle.

Once, he cheated death when his horse bolted while riding in a deer park near Boris. The horse galloped wildly and Arthur's strength began to wane, as he tried desperately to rein in the terrified beast with his two arm stumps. In act of incredible courage, he set it at a seemingly-impossible obstacle, a high brick wall surrounding the estate. As the animal reared, Arthur's saddle device slipped and he was thrown off onto his head. Several hours later, he was found, lying unconscious, by a member of his family.

Arthur trained himself to be a crackshot, using a gun without a trigger guard. He was able to hold the weapon under his left arm stump and squeeze the trigger with the other. He became a skilled yachtsman and a good angler, fishing from a boat or even on horseback. On one of his many travels around the world, he once went deep-sea fishing in the Arctic Circle. He excelled academically and artistically too, becoming a trained draughtsman and a talented painter.

When he was just 15 years old, Arthur, the Limbless Wonder, set out on an arduous tour of Africa and the Middle East as part of his education. Later he became one of the most travelled men of his time, covering vast distances on horseback or being carried by servants.

Once, while sailing down the Nile, Arthur nearly drowned. As his boat rolled suddenly, he was thrown from the deck and was in danger of being crushed by a second vessel alongside as he plunged into the water. None of the party on his boat had witnessed his fall overboard, but an Arab on the riverbank dived in to reach him and managed to bring him ashore. He at first appeared to be dead, but was miraculously revived by artificial respiration.

Only months after Arthur returned from his spectacular youthful adventure, he was planning his next and most ambitious foray. With his tutor, the Reverend David Wood, and his eldest brother Thomas, he set out to travel from Sweden to India on horseback. Their journey was to take them through Finland, Russia, along the Volga, over the Caspian Sea into Persia and, eventually, across the Persian Gulf and into Bombay. It was a three-year expedition which carried Arthur through the ordeals of semi-starvation, bitter winter climates, maddening desert heat and illnesses and hardships that would have proved insurmountable to a lesser man.

In November 1849, Arthur's party met a Persian Prince, whose palace became a temporary home after Arthur developed a fever. He awoke one morning to find himself being nursed back to health by an old black slave in the prince's harem, and spent his convalescence in the ladies' quarters!

In January 1850, he set out again, and once more narrowly cheated death.

Legless acrobat

Legless acrobat Eli Bowen, whose feet were joined straight onto his hips, became a sensation in the early 1900s when he left his home town of Ohio to join the famous circus 'The Greatest Show On Earth' in London. He was able to perform tumbling tricks and nimbly balance at the top of an unsupported pole. By far his most popular act, however, was a joint tandem ride with his geart friend Charlie Tripp – the incredible 'Armless Wonder'!

While crossing 'Old Woman's Pass', the highest in Persia, his horse Jack stumbled and the mule ahead, carrying the party's canteen equipment, struck a rock and vanished over the side of a hidden precipice with a sheer drop of hundreds of feet. A year later, Arthur arrived in Bombay, where he instantly took up a new sport: tiger hunting! He went out in search of big game strapped into the howdah on an elephant's back.

Tragedy struck Arthur's bold expedition when his brother Thomas died of consumption in December 1851. With only 30 shillings left, Arthur was forced to take his first job, at £400 a year, with the East India Company, as a horseback dispatch rider carrying urgent messages. He stayed in employment at Aurumgabad in the Poona district for a year, until he was recalled to Ireland after the death of his elder brother Charles.

Arthur now succeeded to the fabulously rich family estates. And, on 15 March 1855, he was married to his cousin, Frances Mary Leathley, at the home of his aunt in Dublin. The couple had four sons and three daughters. He began on various ambitious local schemes: replanning and rebuilding the entire village of Boris, and opening a railway branch line linking it with the nearby hamlet of Ballyragget, the girlhood home of Anne Boleyn. His new-found flair for civic projects propelled him to further success – as a politician. In 1866 he was elected Member of Parliament for County Wexford, with a majority of 759 votes. In the General Election two years later, he was returned as MP unopposed.

The Limbless Wonder made his maiden speech in the House of Commons from the Opposition benches during a second reading of the Ireland Poor Law Amendment Bill. And to this day he remains the only MP who has ever voted in the House without getting up from his seat to go to the division lobby. Arthur eventually lost his seat in 1880, but was honoured with the appointment as Lord Lieutenant of County Carlow.

Arthur died, after three years of illness, on Christmas Day 1889, and was buried in the small, ruined church at Ballycopigan. His family name lives on, as does the remarkable memory of Arthur MacMurrough Kavanagh himself – the Limbless Wonder who conquered every challenge with a courage which would still humble many able-bodied men.

Say cheese

Say cheese! An amazing man, known only as 'Black Diamond', who was exhibited in Philadelphia in the 19th century, had plenty to smile about as he coined a small fortune from freak show appearances. A rare affliction known as congenital macrostoma had left him with a mouth so abnormally large that his speciality act was to stick both his fists in it at once.

Hervio Nono

O thers born with the tragic misfortune of having no limbs or, hardly better, partially formed stumps where their arms and legs should be, have displayed similar courage to that which took Arthur MacMurrough Kavanagh to the heights of human endeavour and achievement.

The skeleton of Harvey Leach – 'Hervio Nono' as he came to be known – still exists today at University College, London. It shows the figure of a man who must have looked a pathetically deformed sight. His legs were no more than misshapen stumps. His arms too, were gnarled and distorted. His body, which would appear to have been weak though reasonably well-formed, appeared nonetheless squat. His entire body was, indeed, so badly proportioned that when he stood upright, his fingertips touched the ground, wildly exaggerating his tiny lower limbs.

Yet, in his day, Harvey Leach was one of the country's most outstanding gymnasts and seemed, miraculously, to have acquired remarkable power and agility despite his hideous deformities. As an arena horseman, either riding crouched on the animal's back or standing on it, few normally proportioned people were his equal.

Unbelievably, he walked and ran with reasonable ease, and he perfected a breathtaking leap, using both his distorted lower limbs and his arms for propulsion. From sketches made at the time, he is seen to have had a kindly, bearded face, quite handsome, with large, sanguine eyes. To illustrate the enormous difficulties he must have faced – and the enormous courge he must have had to conquer them – the distance between his left hip and heel was 16 inches, while that between his right hip and heel was only 9 inches.

Other Tragic Figures

J ames Leedgwood, of the same era, was born without arms and with only one leg. Yet he was said to be so dextrous with his foot that he could write with it and even use it to fire a hand pistol. In another example of the quite uncanny nimbleness such unfortunate characters seem to have been able throughout history to muster, it was also claimed that the amazing Leedgwood was able to pick up a sewing-needle from a slippery surface while blindfolded!

It still seems a tragedy that many of those unhappy people, were actually exhibited as freaks and objects of fun all over Europe and in America right up until a couple of decades into this century. There is recorded the case of an English boy, who was discovered by a surgeon at the age of 5½, who stood 22½ inches high. He had no legs, just inch-long wads of tissue at the end of his trunk which passed for feet. His right 'arm' was just 2 inches long, his left, 2¼. However, the trunk itself and his head were of perfectly normal proportion for an average boy of his age, giving him a quite strange appearance.

According to the surgeon who found him, he was extremely active, intelligent and had an excellent memory. Indeed, in those attributes, he positively shone for a youngster of his age. He was unable to raise himself into a sitting position from being flat on his back, but if he rested on the lower part of his pelvis he could stay upright.

Surprisingly he was also comparatively mobile – being able to roll himself around by twisting his back to and fro, and he could also pick up objects using his teeth. Unfortunately, as in so many other similar cases, there is no record as to what happened to this brave, resilient child.

In Paris, there was the case of a youth who, although totally armless, learned to play the cornet, using his feet to bring the instrument to his mouth and manoeuvre the keys. He also played the violin with his feet and was able to take a handkerchief from his pocket to blow his nose, roll a cigarette, light it and smoke it, play cards, drink from a glass and eat with a fork. Simple, everyday, routine, dull efforts? Not when you have to perform them all just using your toes.

A celebrated fellow-countryman, who lived a century before in Paris, was Marc Cazotte – known as Pépin to his friends – who lived to the reasonably good age of 62.

He had no arms or legs, but attached to his shoulders on an otherwise perfectly formed trunk were two normal shaped and sized hands. He was renowned, against all the odds, for being extremely graceful and dextrous in his movements.

Marc Cazotte also had a brain to match his graceful style. He was known as something of an intellectual who learned not only to speak but also to write in several languages. Also – and it is a subject most people in his unfortunate state and indeed even the public who were fascinated by him would shy away from – he claimed to lead a normal sex life and was actually rather proud of that fact.

The Man in the Iron Mask

On a bitter winter's night in November 1703, a prisoner in the dreaded Bastille returned to his cell after attending Mass. He had complained to his jailers of feeling unwell and so quickly took to his bed. Within minutes he was dead; his demise so swift that there had been no time for him to receive the sacrament. Just hours later, not only had his body been removed, but all traces of his very existence had been thoroughly and painstakingly wiped away. The thirty years he had spent behind bars vanished as all furniture he had used was burned, all walls and the floor of his cell were meticulously scrubbed and whitewashed – lest he had left a secret written message – and all tiles were removed and replaced. His clothes and few personal possessions were thrown into a furnace. By Royal Decree of King Louis XIV, The Man in The Iron Mask had never existed.

But exist he did; a man whose entire incarceration was a faceless nightmare. A man who, for all that time, was forced to wear a mask under threat of instant execution should he ever try to remove it or reveal in any other way his identity to anyone. Behind bars, he was the man with no name, no face, no past, no future and a present in which he was only ever acknowledged by his captors as simply, 'the prisoner', or, in his later days, 'the ancient prisoner'.

This solitary man, who still captures public imagination as one of the most enigmatic characters of history, became the focus of legends which spread throughout France and then around the world. Theories, even wild rumours, as to his identity remain. Was he, as some say, a dreadfully deformed member of the Royal Household, whose disfigurement was so appalling that Louis ordered him shut away forever to avert shame and scorn being poured on his family? Was he, as others maintain an illegitimate son of the Household, whose face so closely resembled that of Louis that he must never be seen? Was he even the twin brother of Louis, doomed to a faceless limbo-life to preserve the Sun King's glory? One astounding claim put forward is that Louis himself was illegitimate – and that the prisoner was the rightful King of France.

Indeed, remarkable precautions were taken to ensure that no-one ever caught even the slightest glimpse behind the mask. He was always under the control of the same governor, M. de Saint Mars, who moved with him from high-security prison to high-security prison. He was forbidden to associate with other inmates, and guards were under orders to kill him immediately if he tried to talk about anything other than his immediate needs. His name did

The Man In the Iron Mask

not appear on prison records and was never used either verbally or in correspondence. Despite such an incredibly harsh regime, however, he was treated in all other respects like other inmates. His food, clothing and furniture were of good quality. He was allowed his religious rights as a devout Catholic and, apparently, he was always treated and referred to courteously. Indeed, records reveal that King Louis and his ministers constantly inquired about his health and welfare.

The doctor who was allowed to treat him, on the strict condition that he made no attempt to remove the mask, is said to have commented: 'He was admirably made. His skin was dark, his voice interesting.' The only other documented reference to his physical appearance came when M. de Saint Mars, escorting him from the island of St Marguerite to Paris, stopped near Villeneuve. Local people who saw the prisoner said he was tall, well-made, and white-haired. When they dined together, en route to the Bastille, servants noticed that M. de Saint Mars always sat opposite the prisoner, with two loaded pistols by the side of his plate.

Legend – and history itself – has obscured much of what little truth is known about the masked man. The first written references to him appeared in 1761 in the journals of Etienne du Jonca, the King's Lieutenant in the Bastille, who wrote that the prisoner was 'always masked, with a mask of black velvet.' Other sources, however, described the infamous mask as having been made of iron reinforced with steel, with a chin-piece of steel springs to allow the prisoner to eat. It was, of course, on the latter description that Alexandre Dumas based his novel *The Man In The Iron Mask*, although du Jonca was the only eye-witness to provide a written account.

The actual identity of the prisoner, forced to lead as he was a strange, castaway life, remains a mystery. Among possibilities thrown up by historians is the speculation that he may have been a man named Eustache Dauger, who seemingly 'disappeared' after the King expressed dissatisfaction with his behaviour. It appears that Eustache was always in trouble and drifted, before his mysterious vanishing act, towards the darker intrigues of Louis' court, even possibly being involved in devil worship and black masses encouraged by the King's mistress Madame de Montespan.

At one point, around the time of the French Revolution, it was widely believed that the masked man was named Mattioli and that he had been an envoy of the Duke of Mantua who had double-crossed the King in some way.

But for all that, it remains only conjecture; who really was the Man in The Iron Mask? It is said that Louis' great-grandson and successor, Louis XV, on being told the truth about the prisoner, exclaimed: 'If he were still alive I would give him his freedom'. But it appears that the secret was not passed on. Prompted by the curiosity of his wife Marie Antoinette, Louis XVI searched the Royal Archives in vain for details of the man's identity.

Today the legends live on; was this pathetic, hermit-like figure a hideously deformed member of the Royal Family or was he made a tragic outcast because his features so closely resembled those of someone more powerful? Or was he indeed born illegitimately, incurring a wrath which decreed that his face should never, ever fall under public gaze.

The fact is that the Man in The Iron Mask remains what he had always been intended to be: the freak who never was, or at least, was never seen to be.

Freaks of Nature

There are times when a threshold of horror and revulsion is crossed; times when a human freak has to bear, no matter how tragic or pitiable the circumstance, the description of monster. Far beyond the realms even of Edgar Allan Poe, there exist, and have existed, human beings who, by all the laws of nature, should have no rightful place on earth.

Today, a skull is on exhibition at the Royal College of Surgeons in London. It is a skull of two heads which belonged to a child born in Bengal, India, in the last century. The child had been born with a second, supernumerary head, perfect in every feature – eyes, nose, mouth, ears and so on – fused to his own. The heads were joined so that one was actually on top of the other, facing upwards. As an infant, this two-headed boy narrowly escaped death after the midwife who delivered him hurled the nightmarish form in her trembling hands onto a fire.

The child monster survived, and lived for four years. Each head had its own separate blood vessels, brain and, by all accounts, sensibility. The supernumerary head, although firmly fixed in its parasitic position, displayed movement. If its 'host' – and however ludicrous that may sound, it is the only description that seems to fit – was given milk, it would salivate from the mouth. A venomous snake bite killed the boy in infancy, so it can only be left to the imagination to wonder what almost-surreal path his double-headed life would have taken.

His case is, however, not unique. Despite being able to draw only from lay reports, the Victorian medical test *Anomalies and Curiosities of Medicine* does, however, repeat this fairly well documented description:

'One of the weirdest as well as most melancholy stories of human deformity is that of Edward Mordake'. He was heir to one of the noblest peerages in England, yet he never claimed the title, and killed himself at the age of 23. He lived in total isolation, refusing the visits even of the members of his own family. He was an accomplished young man, a profound scholar and a gifted musician. His figure was graceful and his natural face quite handsome. But upon the back of his head was another face, that of a beautiful girl, 'lovely as a dream, hideous as a devil'. The strange parasite face was a mask, occupying an area at the back of the skull, yet exhibiting signs of malignant intelligence. It would sneer and smile while Mordake cried. The eyes would cunningly follow the movements of visitors and the lips would gibber. No voice was audible, but Mordake swore that he was kept from sleeping by the hateful whispers of his 'devil twin', as he called it, 'which never sleeps but talks to me

Pascal Pinon, aged 40 from Lyon, France

forever of such things as they only speak of in hell. No imagination can conceive the dreadful temptations it sets before me. For some unforgiven wickedness of my forefathers I am knit to this fiend – for a fiend it surely is. I beg and beseech you to crush it out of human semblance, even if I die for it.' Such were the words of the hapless Mordake to his physicians.

Despite the close attention of family and doctors, he managed to poison himself, leaving a letter beseeching that the 'demon face' be destroyed before his burial, 'lest it continued its dreadful whisperings in my grave'. He also requested that he be interred on waste ground, without stone or legend to mark his grave.

Quite distinctly apart from Siamese twins, there have been recorded cases of joined infants sharing a single set of limbs. The much-exhibited Tocci brothers, who were born in Turin, Italy, in 1877, each had perfectly formed heads and arms. But below the chest, where they were joined, there was only one pair of legs. It was as if two children were growing up from the base of a single child. The twins, christened Giovanni-Batista and Giacomo, could each control a single leg. Walking was impossible, yet the twins' sensations and emotions above the waist were quite separate and they are believed to have lived well into adulthood.

In Montreal, Canada, in 1878, the case of two female twins, Marie and Rosa Drouin, who shared a single trunk was reported by doctors. Their two upper bodies apparently formed a right-angle to one another. According to one report 'Marie, the left-hand child, was of fair complexion yet more strongly developed than Rosa. The sensations of hunger and thirst were not experienced at the same time, and one might be asleep while the other was crying. They were the products . . . of a mother of 26, whose abdomen was of such preternatural size during pregnancy that she was ashamed to appear in public.' Another case of a single-trunked, double-bodied child is that of the sisters Ritta-Christina, as they were simply known, who were born as Sassari, near Sardinia, on 23 March 1829. As the twins grew into infants, Ritta developed a sad, melancholic character and feeble health while Christina thrived and seemed to be full of happiness.

Monster girl

A two-headed French girl caused a sensation before her death at the age of 12 in 1733 when scientists at the Académie Royale des Sciences in Paris discovered that the supernumerary head could transmit feelings of pain to its partner. When the extra head was pinched, the girl winced and began to cry, with tears streaming down the cheeks of her normal head.

Lazarus-Joannes Baptista Colloredo

Their impoverished parents quickly overcame the traumas of the 'monster-birth' and travelled to Paris hoping to earn a fortune exhibiting them. Forced to stage shows secretly because of prevailing public opinion against such supposedly horrific sights, their clandestine exhibitions were eventually banned by the French authorities and they were soon returning home, penniless once more. The twins did not last long; Rita, the more sickly of the two, expired first and Christina, who had been suckling at her mother's breast, suddenly relaxed and died seconds later with a sigh. Leading physicians anxious to chronicle their case managed to perform a post-mortem examination before the pathetically deformed, mutant body was burned by order of the authorities.

Rare cases of babies born with three heads have been recorded. One such 'monster' was described by a leading expert in deformities in Catania in 1834. Atop an otherwise perfectly normal body, two necks grew from the child. One bore a single head, while from the other grew two further, well-formed heads. All three, it is claimed, functioned normally.

Cases of lifeless, parasite half-bodied growing from otherwise normal people fascinated peep show audiences all over Europe for centuries. One of the most famous was Lazarus-Joannes Baptista Colloredo, from whose trunk hung the upper half of a second body, thought to have been that of a 'twin' which never knew life. Colloredo, born in Genoa in 1617, reached adulthood, carrying his second torso, which seemed to grow out of his stomach, with him to circuses and shows throughout the continent. There were occasional signs of movement in the parasite body, which seemed at times to be trying to breathe. Saliva constantly dribbled from its open mouth, yet its eyes never opened. More common than this extreme example, though, are cases of men and women with three and even four legs.

The Three-Legged Man

When he died in hospital in Jackson, Tennessee on 22 September 1966, Francesco Lentini had created a bizarre record; at 77, he had become the longest-living man ever with three legs.

Lentini, who was billed in later life as the 'Three Legged Wonder', was born at Rosolini, near Syracuse, Sicily, in 1889. His well-to-do parents had twelve other children, five boys and seven girls, who were all shaped perfectly normally. But Lentini, from birth, had an extra leg jutting from the right side of his body. Doctors said it could not be removed surgically, for fear of death or paralysis, and the young boy, condemned to life as an oddity, became, very understandably, chronically depressed and embarrassed as he grew older and more aware of his disability.

When he was seven, his parents took him to an institution for severely handicapped children, where he saw blind, crippled and atrociously deformed youngsters far worse off than himself. 'From that time on,' he cheerfully said later, 'I never complained. I think life is beautiful and I enjoy living it.'

A year later, the family moved to America, where eager circus masters and dime arcade bosses constantly besieged Lentini's father, begging to be allowed to exhibit the boy. His parents refused, insisting that he finish his schooling undisturbed. By the time he did eventually join the Ringling Brothers circus act, Lentini was actually perfectly fluent in four different languages.

Later, he toured with Barnum and Bailey, the Walter Main Circus and Buffalo Bill's Wild West Show in addition to running his own carnival sideshow. He could walk, run, jump, ride a bicycle or a horse, skate on ice or rollers and drive a car. He could not walk on his third limb, however, because it was two inches shorter than his other two but he did learn to kick a ball with it, and developed a wry sense of humour about his abnormality. He would use his third leg as a stool, joking that he was the only man who carried a chair with him everywhere! He claimed he ate 15 per cent more than other men to feed the leg. And he insisted that it was a vital aid when he went swimming, acting as a rudder. Even buying shoes was no problem. He quipped: 'I always buy two pairs and give the extra left one to a one-legged friend!'

Lentini married and had four perfectly normal children. He lived for many years at Weatherfield, Connecticut, moving to sunny Florida in his old age. But he never stopped touring the country and was on the road with the Walter Wanous Side Show when tragically he fell ill and died shortly afterwards.

What was the third leg? As in many other cases, doctors said it was an incomplete Siamese twin. They believed Lentini's mother could have been carrying identical twins, but instead of dividing into two equal parts, her egg only part-divided, leaving Lentini with just the leg of the brother he never had, attached to the base of his spine. According to modern doctors this theory is generally accepted as feasible.

The Four-Legged Woman

The Four-Legged Woman

Another famous multi-limbed freak was Louise L. (her true identity was kept a closely-guarded secret) who toured 19th century France as 'La Dame à Quatre Jambes' – the four-legged woman.

Louise was born in 1869 with two extra, atrophied limbs hanging between her own legs. She always claimed to have feelings in the misshapen limbs, which were about two feet long in adulthood, apart from the feet. Again, doctors believed that the extra legs belonged to a Siamese twin which was never born. Louise, who by all accounts coined a small fortune on the circus circuit, never seemed bothered in private life by her supernumerary appendages. She married and, in the space of three years, gave birth to two perfectly-formed daughters.

Laloo And Others

A dime museum freak who became known only as Laloo, actually had two extra legs, two extra arms and a deformed trunk growing out of his chest. Laloo, who was born in Oudh, India, became famous throughout America in the latter part of the 19th century. And, despite the fact that the parasite body which grew from his was undoubtedly that of an unborn twin brother, he pandered to the whims of peep show managers who dressed it in female clothes to add extra titillation for audiences. A counterpart of Laloo's, who was being exhibited in London around the same time, was a Chinese man known as A-Ke. Casts from his skeleton exist today, and reveal that he had a part-mature foetus growing from his chest, with two arms, two legs and a short trunk.

Duplication of various organs of the body is quite a common occurence – and one which was heavily exploited during the peak of the peep show's popularity in the 19th century. In this area, the sex organs were of special interest to legions of voyeurs in Victorian England; to whom men such as Jean Baptista dos Santos became legendary. It needs little imagination to explain why their following was so large.

THE WORLD'S MOST FANTASTIC FREAKS

Extra ears form the most common casebook; in one 19th century survey of 50,000 children, 33 were found to have at least one additional auricle. An 1870 report in the *British Medical Journal* describes a baby boy born with two perfectly normal ears, plus three extra ones on the right side of his face and two more on the left. By way of home-grown diagnosis the boy's mother claimed that she had been startled during pregnancy by the sight of a child with hideous contractions in the neck!

Double hands have been recorded, as have cases of cloven feet; one 19th century charwoman said her extra hand made an ideal floor rest while she scrubbed away with her other, normal hand, though she maintained that it was less powerful. Multi-fingered hands are common too.

On 16 August 1936, the *Times* newspaper in London carried this report from Mexico City: 'A boy, Modesto Martinez, was born with twenty-five fingers and toes to a family of farmers who have a ranch near Jalapa, capital of Vera Cruz state. The infant has seven fingers on his left hand, six on his right hand and six toes on each foot. An elder brother, Pedro, has twenty-three digits.'

Among the most tragic of all humans are those born with no limbs at all. Indeed, the tremendous courage with which some people, such as 'Limbless Wonder' Arthur Kavanagh, overcome this indescribable burden, is truly inspiring. Today, unhappily, we are well used to the sight of infants born without limbs, an awesome legacy of the Thalidomide drug disaster. Yet many youngsters born limbless have managed to achieve incredible mobility, have learned to write, paint and even play musical instruments in the face of their deformities.

One parallel case of more than a century ago is that of the so-called 'Turtle Woman of Demerara', about whom an article appeared in the medical journal *The Lancet* in 1867. Her thighs were barely six inches long and her distorted feet grew directly from them. Her right arm was a mere stump yet her left one, although grossly misshapen, hung the full length of her body, giving her a bizarre, unbalanced appearance. When she walked, if you can call it that, her strange and stunted ambling gait resembled that of a turtle making slow progress on its route.

She attributed her mutations – as seemed the vogue in those days – to the fact that her mother was frightened during pregnancy by a turtle. Astonishingly, when she was 22 years old, the Turtle Woman gave birth to a normal-sized baby daughter totally free from deformity. She later died of a sex-related disease in the Colonial Hospital.

In contrast to putting limbless yet courageous people on a pedestal in the non-physical sense, in the past this has happened quite literally. The celebrated Violetta, the Victorian 'Trunk Woman' was exhibited on a velvet-topped stand. However sick and degrading that may sound today, she was said – as indeed can be seen from photographs – to have been remarkably pretty and even graceful, with beautifully styled hair and a string of pearls adorning her finely dressed torso.

The Back-To-Front Man

Italian grocer Emilion Guastucci is a walking medical marvel – and that fact once saved his life. Doctors say that there isn't another man in ten million like him. For every organ in his body above the hips is, simply, the wrong way round!

The 63 year old grandfather from Lucca, near Pisa, was born with his heart on the right, his liver on the left, his spleen on the right and so on. Internally, he is a total mirror image of what he should scientifically speaking, look like. It's a good job he is. For, during World War II, when the advancing German Army took over his home town, every remaining healthy man was sent to fight in Russia or Africa.

But when Nazi doctors witnessed Emilion's X-rays, which baffled them completely, they were in a quandary. Should they send him to the front line or deem him unfit for active service? A senior officer reached the decision that he had such a bizarre condition that he could not possibly be allowed to join the fighting and ordered that he should be sent to a hard-labour camp, close to the Austrian border.

What the invaders had not realized, however, was the face that despite his bizarre back-to-front structure – for which medical experts can still not give nor even propose a logical reason – Emilion was, in fact, a perfectly healthy individual.

Within weeks, he managed to escape from incarceration and, calling on almost superhuman reserves, evaded gun patrols to walk home. Emilion was then sheltered from retribution by friends and family and, despite a few heart-stopping moments – felt on the right side of his body, of course, – was never recaptured. From the end of the war, he determined to live life to the full and make his living in the grocery business. Even today, the customers to whom he serves pasta, cheese and bread comment on his peculiar condition and joke: 'Another few slices, please, from the man in ten million.'

THE WORLD'S MOST FANTASTIC FREAKS

Medically, Emilion has a condition called *situs viscerum inversus*, very few other recorded cases of which are to be found around the world. Yet he still enjoys a perfectly normal, ordinary existence. He has two children, a son and a daughter, plus several grandchildren, all of whom are perfectly normal. He says: 'I don't feel any different from anyone else in Italy, even though they first discovered that I was built back-to-front way back in 1933, when I went for my army call-up medical.

'You should have seen the look – an expression you wouldn't believe – on the doctor's face when he discovered that I was not standing back-to-front, or performing some sort of stunt, behind his machine. The German specialists at first simply refused to accept my condition. They didn't believe it was possible.

'It took a series of five more X-rays, before five different doctors until they were finally convinced of the truth. Although I had guessed as much, I was almost as astonished as the doctors at the results of the X-rays. I had always thought that I might, perhaps have been wrongly proportioned – you can't after all, miss a heartbeat on the right instead of the left side of your body – but I never began to realize the full extent of my back-to-frontness.

'All I can really add is that, if God chose me to be different, and created me the wrong-way-round – for some purpose I, certainly, have never been aware, then so be it. I'm in perfectly good health, and I've never really had a problem with illness. So, perhaps, I can even recommend being born back-to-front!'

While Emilion Guastucci may be the original back-to-front man, the circus world and the peep shows of old were delighted when they could recruit those inside-out and upside-down human body tumblers who were expert contortionists and, to give them the medical name in which the Victorians delighted, dislocationists.

Towards the end of the last century, one of the most popular of these characters was the Englishman Wentworth, who, while still performing in his seventies, claimed the title of the world's oldest-ever contortionist. His most popular act was to shut himself, along with six empty soda water bottles in a box measuring a mere 23 by 29 by 16 inches. As he curled his still agile and amazingly flexible body round the bottles, he was packed so tightly in that the lid could be slammed shut on the box. Wentworth even coined a special name for his speciality act: 'Packanatomicalization.'

American contortionist Charles Warren became known as the 'Yankee dish-rag' because of the amazing way in which he could twist his flexible muscles and double joints into virtually any conceivable position. By the tender age of 8, he had joined a travelling troupe of acrobats and strolling performers and within a few years he had tuned his body so perfectly that he could make tiny areas of muscle stand out like a string or perform in a variety of bizarre ways. He was able to contract muscles in his stomach in such a way that vital organs, at will, could be make to bulge out. He could even control the bones of his body to such an extent that, barely moving, he could dislocate his own hip before simply clicking it back into place again. Without any undue effort he could contract his chest to 34 inches and expand it to 41 inches. Warren, a strict teetotaller who weighed in at 150 pounds, could even fool medical experts into believing that he had broken joints or that he had twisted or pulled muscles. He was the father of two children, both of whom could dislocate their hips without breaking into a sweat!

A Frenchman sprang, or rather coiled and twisted, his way to fame around 1886 in his homeland. He was known simply as The Protein Man. He could make his body so completely taut and rigid that hitting him with a hammer had the same effect as trying to bash a concrete wall. Even muscles which in ordinary people are involuntary, he could exercise at will. And he had such power over his body that he could twist himself into what were, in effect, three-dimensional caricatures of figures such as a gnarled old city alderman or a lean and hungry young student.

A leading French scientist who made a detailed study of the Protein Man also discovered that he could totally shut off the blood supply to either side of his body. In other words he could give himself a half-anaemic look by 'switching-off' the supply to the left side of his body and then, in rotation, do the same thing to the right side. The scientist ascribed this weird phenomenon to his ability to control his muscles perfectly.

In Washington in 1893, a man named Fitzgerald claimed his sole source of income was from exhibitions at medical colleges around America. He could simulate every conceivable bone dislocation and became a walking encyclopaedia on the science of pathology. He even claimed to be able to display varying degrees of dislocation which might occur in patients depending what kind of accident had befallen them.

Chapter
Four

The World's Most Famous Siamese Twins

Eng and Chang

There can be no greater bond between human beings than the one made of flesh which links Siamese twins. Today, it is generally a simple surgical task to separate such twins shortly after birth. Yet before medical science made the job an easy one, it was well known for Siamese twins to lead remarkably active lives while joined inescapably together.

The name of this twin freak phenomenon of nature is derived from the brothers Chang and Eng, who were born, firmly meshed together at the chest by a 6-inch-long arm-like band of flesh, to Chinese parents on 11 May 1811, in the province of Meklong, Siam. Almost at once, they were decreed an omen of disaster by the King of Siam, who ordered them killed before they could wreak their supposedly mystical havoc. In what was to become a stroke of good fortune for not only Chang and Eng themselves, but for paying voyeurs and peep show bosses the world over, the King did, eventually, relent and allowed a Scottish merchant called Robert Hunter to take the inseparable infants to America.

From birth, there had been an enormous gulf in the health of the twins; Eng, enfeebled and sometimes struggling just to survive, Chang, thriving and with a seeming thirst for life. These traits were not only reflected later in life by their health but also by their characteristics. As they grew older Chang increasingly developed a taste for American bourbon and any other alcoholic beverage. Eng abhorred drunkenness. Chang, not surprisingly, grew violent after his boozing bouts, and he only escaped being sent to prison for assault because a judge thought it would be grossly unfair to have to incarcerate the peacable Eng with him!

Despite their psychological differences, however, Chang and Eng became a global sensation; first America and then the world marvelled – after paying the entrance fee – at the living and bonded mirror image twins. In virtually every country they toured, a fierce debate ensued among leading medical experts as to whether or not they could be separated. In France, they sparked even greater controversy when their exhibition was banned on the grounds that they would create monsters by making an evil impression on pregnant women. In the heyday of the peep show, Chang and Eng reigned supreme as the exhibits most likely to cause a storm wherever they went. The amount of information about them in the Surgeon-General's library in Washington that survives today is truly remarkable. It seemed the whole world was talking about them, anxious to catch just a glimpse of the original Siamese twins.

Eng and Chang

THE WORLD'S MOST FANTASTIC FREAKS

At the end of their mammoth European tour, which included a visit to London in November 1829, they decided to bow out of public life and, their Westernization complete, settled down as farmers in North Carolina using the name of Bunker. At the age of 44, they married two expatriate English sisters, Sarah Ann and Adelaide Yates, respectively 26 and 28 years old, and, sharing what was perhaps understatedly described as a 'very large bed', sired between them twenty-one children, all of whom were born healthy. To allay Deep South American primness and priggishness, which at the time demanded domestic fidelity whatever the cost, they eventually stationed their wives in different houses, and visited each in turn for a week at a time. Quite astonishingly, they never fell victim to the salacious 'yellow journalism' which thrived then as it exists now. They were, by all accounts, left, if not entirely in peace, with slightly more than a modicum of self-respect and led a quiet life, well away from the glare of the peep show circuit.

In 1869, Chang and Eng returned to Europe. They were on a mission to consult the leading surgeons of Britain and France on the advisability of being separated. It is claimed that, after a fierce quarrel, they felt such hatred towards each other that they wanted to be surgically separated. More likely, they were broke – and needed to exhibit and advertise themselves in an effort to raise extra cash. The truth is perhaps best illustrated in a description which states: 'A most pathetic characteristic of these illustrious brothers was the affection and forbearance they showed for each other until shortly before their death. They bore each other's trials and petty maladies with the greatest sympathy, and in this manner rendered their lives far more agreeable than a casual observer would suppose possible.'

On 17 January 1874, Chang and Eng died. An autopsy was performed yet the belief remains that they both died simultaneously of old age. Skilled surgeons examined their connected bodies, dissected the flesh bond which joined them and speculated as to the medical background of their co-existence. They remain, however, both enigmatic and contemporary; they were the original Siamese twins.

Masha and Dasha

Russian Siamese twins Masha and Dasha really are like chalk and cheese. The little sisters, joined at the pelvis, are almost total opposites, despite the fact that they dance, ride a bicycle and even climb ladders together. Masha is said to be 'a lightweight chatterbox who flirts with boys', while Dasha is deeply serious and studious. They each have one leg under their own control and there is a third, lifeless one in which neither one feels sensation.

The Biddenden Twins

Britain's first and most celebrated Siamese twins, although they were not then known as such, were 'Ye Maydes of Biddenden'. They were born, in Biddenden, Kent, around 1100; allegedly joined together at both the hips and the shoulders. Today they are still remembered by local custom on Easter Monday, when locals in the small village bake Biddenden Maid cakes.

According more to legend than documented fact, Eliza and Mary Chulkhurst, the Maids, lived for thirty-four years and, as one died, the other declared 'As we came together we will also go together', and expired six hours later. It is claimed that they bequeathed to the church wardens of their parish a large estate of more than 20 acres. Actual credibility is always obscured by legend, yet such a death-bed land transaction is, although obliquely, noted in local records. One record states: 'It is not safe to say that such an anomaly is impossible'. Another refers to church officials 'Using their wands for purposes other than of office' to counteract the supposed effect of two joined together members of their congregation. Whatever the truth, it remains a distinct likelihood that pygopagous twins – to give them their clinical definition – did exist in Biddenden, near Staplehurst, Kent, around the dawning of the 12th century.

Other Famous Twins

The little Jones brothers, born in Tipton County, Indiana on 24 June 1889, became the first recorded case of twins joined together by their spinal columns. At birth they weighed a healthy enough 12 pounds and were 22 inches long. Apart from the long, tube-like shared spine, all their other features were normal although, uncharacteristically, they differed in complexion and hair and eye colourings.

Somewhat startlingly, they became freak show exhibits when they were only a few months old. Records reveal that they went on show at St John's Hotel in Buffalo right up to their deaths on 19 and 20 February 1891. They were then less than two years old and had been public property virtually since they had been born.

The old saying goes that two's company and three's a crowd. But for some people, three has to be company . . . when one Siamese twin falls in love and marries.

It happened to Rosa and Josefa Blazek, born joined together at the lower back and pelvis in Czechoslovakia in 1880. They had two hearts, two pairs of lungs, but only one stomach. Rosa met and married a German officer and had his baby, a boy called Franz, who was 7 when his father died in 1915 during World War I.

Hiltons

Daisy and Violet Hilton, joined together at the spine, were among England's most celebrated Siamese twins. Heads turned and people stopped to stare at the sight the picture here shows of the twins returning to their homeland in January 1933 after an absence of 22 years in America. Their visit was marked by a celebration, for Miss Daisy had just announced her engagement.

THE WORLD'S MOST FANTASTIC FREAKS

The sisters were said to have two distinct personalities, each with their own idiosyncrasies and tastes. Rosa drank only wine, her twin preferred beer and the mixture regularly upset their stomach! They are also said to have argued frequently, but they managed to bury their differences long enough to earn what in those days was a staggering £45,000 from touring peep shows first in Europe and then America, before Josefa contracted jaundice in Chicago.

Rosa ate in an effort to keep her twin's strength up as she lay ill, but resolutely refused to allow surgeons to separate them, saying: 'If Josefa dies, I want to die too.' In 1922, she did die, only 15 minutes after her twin.

The problem of one Siamese twin wanting to marry also caused problems for Margaret and Mary Gibb. Margaret eventually married 21-year-old Mexican college graduate Carlos Josefe at Newark, New York, in 1929 after long agonizing over whether she should take the plunge with sister Mary. The girls, then 18, were joined at the base of the spine and had dismissed marriage as an impossibility when they were young.

Margaret told newspaper reporters: 'I told my sister how I felt about Carlos, yet it still seemed impossible that I could marry him, even if he were willing to marry me. It was then that my sister suggested a possible way out of the dilemma. Despite the risk of death, she urged that we should undergo a separation operation so that I could be married in the normal way. We sought the advice of an eminent surgeon, who said it could not be done, since it would certainly result in the death of one if not both of us because our arterial and nervous systems are linked. We therefore decided that I should get married as I am – rather than lose my great chance of happiness.'

The girls, both attractive brunettes, learned to cope with life together, even as a new threesome. Margaret said: 'Mary and I can do nearly everything in the household, including baking and making pies. We can also dance, sing and play the piano and the ukelele!'

It must be a truly bitter-sweet moment when Siamese twins are separated. Bitter, perhaps, because that unique bond created by nature has been severed for ever and with it the sometimes almost total empathy such twins so often seem to share. Sweet, certainly, because that bond – the one made of flesh – can be an imprisoning chain-link which restricts the freedom of movement, indeed, freedom to live anything like a normal life, of both people.

Even in the early decades of this century, separation operations were considered, even when the connection between the two bodies did not involve any vital organs, to be highly dangerous. (A century before this, any reluctance was rather more because of superstition; it was felt wrong to tamper with such acts of God and nature.) Today, however, separation operations are reasonably common; in fact, it has become surprisingly rare to hear of cases of still-joined Siamese twins reaching any great age beyond

---

Strong swimmer

Swimming strong-man Tom Rice startled onlookers in San Francisco Bay on 9 August 1979, who believed they were watching a newly constructed 200-ton replica of Sir Francis Drake's ship, the *Golden Hind* , sailing away without a crew. In fact Rice, wearing swim fins, was actually pulling it!

---

infancy or childhood because such an operation, in their case, has not been possible on medical grounds.

One of the most heart-warming recent separations was that of the Beaver twins – Fonda Michelle and Shannon Elaine – in Forest City, USA at the age of 2. Certainly, it was heart-warming for their mother Kim, whose words to newspaper reporters a few months after completion of the operation were: 'They're walking! My babies are really walking! My God, I'm the proudest mother in the whole wide world.' The irony behind her ecstatic words is that, when joined, her little girls had only two legs between them. Now, separated, they have, of course, only one leg each. But, almost miraculously, only a few months after the operation, and with a minimum amount of therapy, they were actually both taking their first faltering steps. Their paces may have been only a few inches at a time, but to their mother, the twins were taking giant strides in courage and determination.

The little toddlers, who were born on 9 February 1980, joined at the pelvis, travel each day to the Rutherford Hospital near their home for physical therapy and to walk between parallel bars. At home now, they can stand unassisted, and quite happily push along toy carts while Kim and her husband Arlin, aged 22, watch with growing joy as each day they grow stronger and more confident and independent in their desires to keep walking until they have mastered the art completely.

Arlin delightedly told journalists: 'Who wouldn't be proud of having such super kids? Their progress has been marvellous. We hardly dared to hope that they would do so well, but their courage and determination has been amazing. Tests indicate that mentally they are above the norms for their age. Each day they seem to learn a whole new bunch of words and they chatter away to each other. We're confident that they can build happy, successful lives – just look at the start they've made!'

Kim agreed: 'Never for one moment have I regretted their birth. They are special, wonderful, adorable babies. They are so sweet and good despite all their problems. Sometimes it's difficult to express just how much we love them. We really and truly feel blessed to have such wonderful babies. To see them develop and change each day is a tremendous privilege. You see, they're going to make it. They're winners, not losers. Those big hearts they have will see them through. No matter what hurdles are in the way, I know these wonderful kids are going to overcome them.' Certainly, the indomitable fighting spirit of the youngsters gives their parents good cause to be proud. They never cry if they fall over – the one left standing rags the other to get back up and join her.

Doctors share the family's confidence that Fonda Michelle and Shannon Elaine are poised to progress in leaps and bounds, as indeed they have done to date, until they are both capable of walking any distance freely themselves.

Though operations to separate Siamese twins were quite rare a century or so ago, there is one amazing historical record of such an operation being performed as early as AD 945. Two small boys who were joined at the abdomen were brought from Armenia to Constantinople for public exhibition. After being on display for some time in what really must have been an ancient forerunner of the sort of freak show that was to achieve such popularity throughout Europe centuries later, they were ordered to be removed by the government, which believed, though it had taken a fair amount of time to come to its decision, that they were harbingers of evil.

The twins, however, did return at the beginning of the reign of Constantiner VII, when again, to sate popular demand, they were put on public show. Tragically, though, one of them died and, in a desperate effort to keep the other alive, surgeons performed a primitive operation to part them. Miraculously, it was a success, despite the fact that the separated twin also died three days later, pining for his brother.

A much later attempt at separation was made in 1881 when surgeons did manage to separate two Swiss sisters, Marie and Adele, just over four months after their birth. Tragically though, the infants were sickly, and Adele died six hours after the operation. Marie survived for another 24 hours, but then she died too, suffering from peritonitis.

As with freak shows, 19th century surgery did, on occasion, tend to be regarded as a spectator sport to be shared by all, and pioneering operations or those involving particularly famous or infamous characters tended to be carried out with an attendant blaze of publicity.

So it was when the eminent Parisian doctor Doyen – who became known, somewhat unkindly, in various newspapers of the time as 'the Barnum of surgery' – decided to try to separate the famous Orissa Sisters. The sisters, Radica and Doddica, had been born in India in 1889. When they were 4 years old they went to Europe and later on, still joined by a band which connected their livers, entered the tinselled world of peep-showbusiness and went on tour.

THE WORLD'S MOST FAMOUS SIAMESE TWINS

Dr Doyen's determination to separate the little sisters attracted the attention of showmasters all over Europe, as well as newspapers, who were anxious, in the time-honoured tradition, to carve themselves a slice of the action. One promoter put forward the idea, which was accepted, that the operation itself should be performed in the Cirque de Paris as the drum-rolling climax to a charity circus show gala evening aimed at raising funds to be used by the Orissa Sisters once they were apart.

Although television has made us quite used to watching delicate surgery being performed, it is believed that this was the first occasion when attendant cameras – early stills cameras, of course – were there to record every cut and thrust of the scalpel. In the expectant hush, Dr. Doyen prepared to make his first incision. Then, as he began to cut, the flash powder puffed, the cameramen made sure they had their angle right, the promoter looked anxiously on, the audience gasped, and the little Orissa Sisters died.

Chapter
Five

Hair!

The Wolf Boy and other hair-raising freaks

In a land of 900 million people, little Yu Chenhuan is a medical marvel. When he was born in 1977, to peasant parents in the remote Chinese province of Liaoning, doctors were baffled by the long, silky hair which grew in a fine line down his spine.

They were certain it would quickly disappear. But instead, it kept on growing at a phenomenal rate, and within weeks covered Yu's entire body. Soon, his face was so hairy that he became known for hundreds of miles around as the 'Wolf Boy' and his astonished mother and father found themselves keeping his beard in trim in between bottle-feeding him. Despite a year of tests and experiments, Chinese scientists were forced to admit that they couldn't find a cure. Today, the hair still continues to grow. Yu, now a young boy, sports a full set of whiskers on his face and a dark, furry down still covers his entire body.

Bearded Ladies

Other hair-raising cases of extreme hirsuteness have exasperated the experts and amazed audiences all over the world – but none more so than those involving bearded ladies. The whiskers of Kentucky's famous bearded lady Janice Deveree, which earned her a fortune from dime arcades and peep shows, were measured as a flowing 14 inches at the height of her career in 1884, when she was 42 years old. A Swiss lady, Madame Fortune Clofullia, was showered with diamonds by Emperor Napoleon III who was delighted, much to the annoyance of the Empress, that she styled her beard the same way he did his. The fortunate Madame Fortune coined further riches when she joined Phineas T. Barnum's freak show circuit in America and drew more than 3½ million paying customers in just nine months.

Eventually she married an artist and had two children; first a girl and then a boy who became almost as hairy as she was Her son was, in fact, exhibited alongside her by Barnum, whose advertising posters declared: 'His body is

Yu Chenhuan

THE WORLD'S MOST FANTASTIC FREAKS

Annie Jones-Elliot appeared with the Barnum and Bailey Circus from her childhood on.

Longest moustache

Holy whiskers! The world's longest moustache was cultivated by Indian religious man Masuriya Din. It sprouted to a staggering length of 8 feet 6 inches between 1949 and 1962. He is on the verge of being rivalled by New Delhi prisoner Karna Ram Bheel, who in 1979 was granted permission by his jail governor to keep the 7 feet 10 inch top-lip growth he hopes will eventually win him the record.

thoroughly covered with hair, more particularly over the shoulders and on the back; his face is fully surrounded with whiskers, fully marked and about half an inch in length, but of light colour. The child is strong and healthy and promises fair to astonish the reader.'

Perhaps the most astonishing thing about Madame Fortune's son was the fact that, under the showname 'Infant Esau', he was exhibited wearing dresses until he was 14 years old. This was typical Barnum hokum; not satisfied with a bearded boy, he did his best to dupe punters into believing that they were actually viewing a bearded girl!

One of the earliest recorded bearded ladies who was put on show was Rosine-Marguerite Muller, who became a celebrated 18th century circus attraction in her native Germany and died, with a thick beard and heavy moustache, in hospital in Dresden in 1732. A century later another bearded lady, Julia Pastrana, was so bewhiskered and hairy that she was billed as 'The Ugliest Woman in the World.'

Julia married her manager, a man called Lent, and their union is said to have been blessed (or cursed) with a daughter so akin to her mother in ugliness, that, at the sight of her, Julia was so distraught that she died soon afterwards. The bizarre story went on when Lent not only continued to exhibit her after her death – in mummified form – but also discovered another bearded girl, whom he persuaded to change her name to Pastrana, and displayed her as his wife's living sister.

Lent eventually married his new discovery and so established a record for himself as the only man to have wed two bearded women. Victorian physicians George Gould and Walter Pyle chronicled a 'curious case of a woman of 23 (Mrs Viola M.), who from the age of three had a considerable quantity of hair on the side of the cheek which eventually became a full beard. She was quite feminine and was free from excessive hair elsewhere, her nose and forehead being singularly bare. Her voice was very sweet; she was married at 17½, having two normal children and nursed each for one month.'

Other Hair Raising Freaks

J o-Jo the Dog-faced Boy and Lionel the Lion-faced Man were two of the most popular peep show attractions throughout Europe in the 19th century. Jo-Jo is said to have resembled a Skye terrier because of the silky yellow hair which entirely covered his face and grew in two especially thick tufts either side of his nose.

His fame as an 'animal freak' was accompanied with graphic tales of his capture as a feral child in the virgin forests of Russia, where he was said to have lived on berries and small animals which he learned to hunt from his wolf neighbours. The story is sheer hogwash, for Jo-Jo is known to have grown up around the circuses and fairgrounds of Europe, where his act involved imitating a wild, snapping dog; behaviour stage-managed to fit his undeniably canine face.

Similarly, Lionel, whose face was totally covered by long, mane-like hair, learned to improve his act and terrify his audiences by roaring and snarling as soon as the curtain was raised. Jo-Jo and Lionel had actually been baptized Feodor Jeftichew and Stephen Bibrowsky respectively. On realizing the vast potential their extreme hirsuteness opened up to them, and in the true traditions of what, after all, was a thriving branch of showbusiness, they quickly changed their names legally to those more in keeping with their appearances.

Lady Olga

Lady Olga, whose real name was Jane Barnell had the longest beard ever exhibited by a woman. She sported a full moustache and her beard was, in fact, thirteen and a half inches long. She also bore the proud distinction of having had a longer career in the side shows than any other woman.

Despite her beard and whiskers, Lady Olga did marry and gave birth to four children. This was not at all uncommon. As far as can be ascertained, nearly all the famous bearded ladies were married.

Unfortunately, Lady Olga, was probably not happy in her role as a side show attraction, despite her tremendous success. She was prone to sudden swings in her mood, ranging from good humour to extreme temper tantrums, probably aggravated by her weakness for alcohol.

Julia Pastrana

Lionel

Longest hair

Lady Godiva could never have matched this! Swami Pandarasannadhi, head of the Tirudadutuari monastery in Madras, India was in 1949 – and still is – the record holder for the world's longest hair. It then measured an almost unbelievable 26 feet from his head to the ends, stretching way behind him.

At least one hairy freak has been born to royalty; Margaret of Parma, who was Regent of the Netherlands from 1599 to 1667, was a blue-blooded bearded lady. It is also documented that King Charles XII of Sweden had a bearded female grenadier in his army who was captured by advancing Russian troops during the Battle of Poltava in 1709 and taken to the Tsar's court as a curiosity.

The most famous diarist in history, Samuel Pepys, perhaps best illustrates the curiosity such hair-raising freaks arouse with his entry for 21 December 1668:

'I went into Holborne (London's Holborn) and there saw a plain little woman . . . her voice like a little girl's, with a beard as much as I ever saw a man with, almost black and grizly . . . bushy and thick. It was a mighty strange sight to me, I confess . . . and pleased me mightily.'

One of the most popular freak show troupes in Victorian England was the 'Seven Sutherland Sisters', all of whom had hair which literally trailed behind them on the ground. Their trellised locks earned them fame and fortune towards the latter end of the 19th century; whether or not they actually all were sisters is uncertain. What is for sure is that their hair colourings were not the same and so, when exhibited, their flowing carpet of hair must have had something of a stunning rainbow effect.

Extreme hair length seemed to be common during the era and not only in freak shows. A London doctor recorded the case of a woman aged 38 whose locks touched the floor and when measured, proved to be an astonishing 5 feet 5 inches in length.

It was an era too, when men prided themselves on sporting long, often elaborately trimmed and coiffed beards. One of the most famous documented figures of the time was Louis Coulon, whose set of whiskers measured an astonishing 11 feet. One picture of him shows a black cat sitting in the 'nest' his beard formed after it was draped around his shoulders several times as it had to be to enable him not only to walk without tripping over it, but also to display a chestful of medals he proudly wore.

Even he, however, was beaten by a whisker in the super-beard stakes by a businessman from Northern France called Jules Dumont, whose hairy growth from the chin measured a staggering 12 feet. His beard flowed into two separate channels of hair and so made an impressive sight when stretched out in full. This was only possible when Dumont walked backwards to display its total length. Again, had he tried confidently marching forwards, he would have tripped over his twin rivers of beard.

It is worth comparing these amazing beards with the record growth of a horse mane, which was only 12 inches longer than Dumont's! Many freaks, self-styled, did of course combine excessive hair growth with excessive beard growth, completing the total 'hairy monster' image which was ever-popular during the era, quite distinctly from the 'wild man' exhibits. Bearded women, especially, added to their public allure by letting their hair grow to inordinate lengths and so promoting the confusing male/female appearance so beloved by their keen and paying customers.

Extremely hairy native tribes (from which, allegedly, came many of the 'wild' men and boys who went on exhibition) also evoked considerable interest during the period. One which came under the sharp focus of the medical and quasi-medical media of the time was the Hairy Ainu tribe, now a dying race found mainly on islands off Japan. The Hairy Ainu are tall, extremely well-developed muscularly and incredibly – as the name might suggest – hairy. It is an irony that they should be found close to the smooth-skinned people of Japan itself, among whom excessive hirsuteness is a rarity. Their tribesmen are still hunters, and, under the terms of their wierd religion, worship the bear above all else. No longer a totally pure race, having inter-mingled over the years with the Japanese, they are today in the throes of becoming extinct.

Oriental gurus and mystics are also renowned, even in modern times, for cultivating long, trailing beards and hair. In many cases, extreme hairiness is hereditary, as is perhaps best exemplified by a famous Victorian picture of four members of a Burmese family, two of whom not only have long hair but

---

Longest beard

The world's longest beard was worn by Norwegian-born Hans Langseth, who quit the American circus circuit because he was so fed-up with people tugging his whiskers, which had taken 59 years to grow and trailed an astonishing 17½ feet, to make sure they were genuine. On his death at the age of 81, a relative cut off the beard and kept it in a trunk for 40 years, before donating it to the Smithsonian Institute in Washington where it remains to this day.

Burmese hairy family

also beards which are so full that their faces are almost obscured by whiskers, well in keeping with the traditions of their freak show contemporaries Jo-Jo and Lionel, who were similarly 'masked'.

Hairy Tales

One of the best-known and often discussed hair-raising tales is of how hair can, even in a very young person turn from its natural colour to white overnight. A record dating back to 1546 relates the story of a young man who was thrown into jail for seducing his girl companion. Expecting the death sentence, he appeared before a judge the following day with grey-white hair and beard. His colouring had been dark the night before!

The story ends happily for the man, who was scared white and witless, for in court the very sight of him provoked pity, and he was granted a pardon. Also on record is the case of a clergyman's daughter from Nottingham, who awoke one morning to find a pure white spot of about one-and-a-half inches on the crown of her previously totally jet-black hair. In an astonishing series of overnight changes, her hair soon became striped white, giving her a quite alarming 'zebra girl' effect. Her hair continued undergoing its strange, spasmodic metamorphosis, and within seven years it was totally white, although she was still only 20 years old.

Another girl, Maria Seeley from Bedfordshire, experienced the same incredible 'two-tone' effect. Although she was only 8 years old, her hair grew long and dark on one side, but remained light and short on the other. Similarly, one side of the little girl's body was brown-skinned, while the other side was fair. Doctors were uncertain as to what could have caused her astounding split-image effect. Even experts in London failed to ascertain the reason for it; certainly she had not had any sort of severe fright or undergone any undue emotional stress. The case remaines a total mystery.

In a collection of similar bizarre occurrences which was published in a scientific magazine in October 1890 is that of an American in 1851, who was sleeping alone at night in a camp. The man, aged 51, was terrified on awakening by the sight of a grizzly bear. It was a sight which, apparently, scared him totally white in a single day. A 23-year-old Californian gambler suffered a similar fate but for an entirely different reason. His adrenalin must have been pumping at a phenomenal rate when he placed 1,100 dollars – his entire life savings – on the turn of a single card. As the card was being dealt he was seen to be in a state of extreme nervous excitement. The next day, he had white hair. (Unfortunately there is no actual record of whether he won or lost. Presumably, if it was the former, he was thereafter quite happy to live with the look of his locks!)

There have been a number of cases reported of hair turning white, and then reverting again just as suddenly and mysteriously to its natural shade. One is that of a 36-year-old woman whose raven-black hair began to turn white, on the 23rd day of a malignant fever. After 29 days, her hair was perfectly white, but just a day after that it began, strangely, to darken. A week further on, it had completely reverted to its former colour, as black even at the roots as it had ever been.

Chapter
Six

Skin Deep

Luminous People

Electrical power is one of man's greatest creations. Harnessing it has given us unprecedented sophistication in both home and industrial life. But not all electricity comes from burning coal, gas or oil, from nuclear reactors or hydro-electric plants. Doctors and scientists have found yet another, confounding source – the human body itself. There are people who can glow in the dark and others who can disrupt – or mysteriously activate – electric currents.

Religious tracts have always told of auras or halos appearing around or over holy men. But there are also records of secular folk who shine and shimmer with no claim to ecclesiastical fame. A letter published in *English Mechanic* magazine in September 1869, related the tale of an American woman who, 'on going to bed, found that a light was issuing from the upper side of the fourth toe of her right foot. Rubbing increased the phosphorescent glow and it spread up her foot. Fumes were also given off, making the room disagreeable; and both light and fumes continued when the foot was held in a basin of water, or scrubbed with soap. It lasted for 45 minutes before fading away, and was witnessed by her husband.'

In May 1934, the astonishing case of Anna Morano brought leading doctors and specialists flocking to her bedside in Pirano, Italy. Signora Morano suffered from asthma. But no-one could begin to explain why, for several months, her breasts emitted a clearly visible blue glow while she slept. Her heart rate doubled while this happened, yet the glow was not caused by her sweat. Indeed she perspired only after each strange emission.

Three years later, two eminent British doctors documented the case of a female patient with breast cancer whose affected flesh gave off a light so bright that it could illuminate the hands of a watch several feet away in the dark. Infants, too, occasionally emit a soft, white radiance. One boy, born in Saint-Urbain, France, in 1869, was seen by witnesses to shoot luminous rays

---

Drip-die

The astonishing case of the 'Drip-Die Man' was reported in the *Medical and Physical Journal* of London on 25 February 1885. A 77-year-old-man, of previously good health, began to sweat profusely for no apparent reason, and continued to do so until he died of exhaustion after three months of continual perspiration.

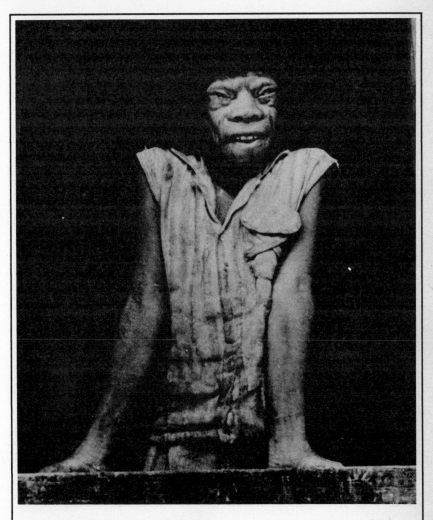

South American Mystery

Maria de Jesus, born in 1964, lives in Belo Horizonte in the Gerais state of Brazil. She is a mystery to all scientific and medical specialists, none of whom have been able to explain the paradox of this girl, who has more characteristics of a simian than a human being.

from the ends of his fingers. The child, bathed in light when he died, also badly shocked all who tried to touch him. He was just nine months old.

Angelique Cottin was only 14 when her ten-week ordeal as an 'electric person' began in her home town of La Perrière on 14 January 1846. Objects seemed to retreat from her whenever she went near them. Her slightest touch was enough to send furniture careering across the room, spinning wildly or jumping up and down. No-one could hold onto anything already in her grasp. Compasses were sent wild whenever she was near. Yet this was no eerie poltergeist. Doctors could only attribute her unseen power to the fact that her heartbeat rose to 120 a minute in the evening, during which time her electro-magnetic power seemed to increase and centre, for no apparent reason, on her left forearm.

Jennie Morgan was another teenager to suffer what in today's cliché-ridden world of science might be termed 'High Voltage Syndrome'. During the 1890s, witnesses attest, actual sparks flew from her to nearby objects at her home in Sedalia, Missouri. Animals shunned her, and some people who shook her hand were knocked unconscious, supposedly by shock waves. In London, 20 years earlier, 18-year-old Caroline Clare had, according to record, been terrified when ordinary household cutlery stuck to her skin. Even the stays on her corset are said to have become magnetized.

The phenomenon of luminosity and super-static powers is not, of course, an exclusively female affliction. In 1889, doctors intensively studied the case of Frank McKinstry of Joplin, Missouri, whose feet stuck immovably to the ground when he became 'highly-charged'. And in 1890, Maryland scientists were completely dumbfounded by the wierd powers of Louis Hamburger, who could lift a 5 pound jar of iron filings with the tips of three fingers. Eight years previously, a Zulu boy was exhibited in Edinburgh, for giving off intense electrical shocks.

The 20th century too, has its share of electric people. In 1920, doctors at Clinton Prison, New York, published a paper reporting on 34 convicts who had suffered from botulinus poisoning. Amazingly, compasses could not work in their presence and metal objects simply moved – as if by some dark

Conductor

American forest ranger Roy Sullivan, of Virginia, is a human lightning conductor. He is the only man alive to have been struck seven times – between 1942 and 1977 – and survive. Lightning bolts have burned off his hair, eyebrows and big toenail, and his chest, stomach, legs, shoulder and ankle have all been scorched.

and mysterious form of auto-suggestion – away from them. Paper, also, seemed to be affected, and stuck to their hands. When they recovered from the poisoning however, the high-voltage symptoms seemed to vanish too.

The Super Static Girl

Perhaps the best documented case of human electro-magnetism recorded is that of Anne-Marie Schneider at Rosenheim, Bavaria. Police, top scientists and leading engineers from both the electricity and telephone authorities were called in after a series of bizarre events at the offices of a lawyer in November 1967. Yet they could find no logical explanation of why 8-foot-long strip-lighting fitments unscrewed themselves from the ceiling, why electronic alarm switches were tripped for no reason, why four telephones rang when no-one was on any of the lines and why chemical liquids in a photocopying machine poured from their containers.

It was left to Professor Hans Bender, Director of the Institute for the Frontiers of Psychology at Freiburg-im-Breisgau, to discover that such inexplicable electrical mischief only happened when 19-year-old Anne-Marie, a clerk-secretary, was in the office. Identical phenomena occurred when she was sent home, and even when she changed jobs. When she visited a bowling alley managed by her fiancé, electrical equipment at the establishment went haywire.

Studies by two psychologists from the Max Plauck Institute of Plasmaphysics in Munich-Garching discovered that Anne-Marie could absorb electrical power both from direct-current mains and from batteries. She could also provide – simply from her body – a ten-volt power signal on a microphone when no sound was audible. Currents of 50 ampères were recorded on hypersensitive measuring instruments when she was near – and no conventional power source was switched on. Light bulbs swayed wildly and then dimmed as Anne-Marie walked by. And, staggeringly, it was discoverd that she could call the correct number for the telephone time answering service five times in a minute without even touching the dial.

Experts found that her ability to emit long-distance electrical impulses, linked apparently to a high level of clairvoyance, coincided with states of intense hyper-tension. Yet they could not explain how Anne-Marie had achieved her extraordinary mental power as a natural super-static person.

Eddie Mae Kearney

Freak Skin

The old saying goes that a leopard cannot change its spots. Another says that beauty is only skin deep. Whatever the case, freak skin disorders – 'desperate, but not serious,' as the Victorian physicians would have it – have claimed hundreds of victims, many of whom in times gone by have made their fortunes from the circus and the peep show.

Among the most popular of these have been part-albino negroes, or 'pied blacks' as they were called, whose bodies resembled those of Dalmatian dogs with a mass of mottled black-on-white or white-on-black spots. An engraving of a little boy from the Caribbean called George Alexander, was published in 1809, showing him at play with a spotted dog. With such children and animals, it was the rather unkind advertising boast of circus masters, it was difficult to tell the two apart.

New Yorker Eddie Mae Kearney is shown here in a 1981 photograph. It was taken shortly after her skin began its uncanny reversal process. A pigmentation disorder caused it to turn from black to white in 1959. Just over 20 years later, it began to revert back to black, leaving her arms and legs with the 'Dalmation' effect which is strikingly illustrated.

Among the most celebrated of Victorian freaks was Felix Wehrle who had – like 'India Rubber Man' James Morris – skin which was so abnormally elastic that he could stretch whole fistfuls of it inches away from his body without damaging it. Wehrle, who was also so double-jointed that he could bend his fingers backwards and forwards at alarming angles, became known, not surprisingly, as the 'Elastic Skin Man'.

Experts discovered that, unlike cases of congenital skin deformity, Wehrle's bendable and twistable tissue did not hang loosely or in folds. He is said to have been able to pull a clump of skin from any part of his body, even his face, to a distance of six inches or more, and then let it simply twang back into place.

A rival of Wehrle's was a Ceylonese performer called Rhannin, who pulled in enormous crowds at London's Alhambra music hall, where he was billed as 'The Man With The Iron Skin'. His act aimed to prove that his skin was impervious to any kind of sharp metal point. Indeed, the highlight of his show involved clambering through a tight metal ring with spikes pointing inwards and then emerging without a scratch.

For the purposes of publicity, Rhannin claimed that he had discovered a miracle elixir which made his skin impregnable. As his fame spread, medical experts proposed the theory that Rhannin was, in fact, a fakir who, after long practice and intense mental concentration, had hardened his body against pain. Professors at the Berlin clinic decided however, after a series of lectures to discuss his case, that his super-resistant skin was a totally inexplicable phenomenon.

Modern-day fakirs still profess to have the power to lie on a bed of nails or walk on hot coals without feeling pain. But, astonishingly, the world record for lying on a bed of nails belongs to a vicar from Wales.

According to the *Guinness Book of Records,* the Reverend Ken Owen spent 102 hours 23½ minutes on his back on a board covered with 6-inch nails, placed 2 inches apart, in a charity fund-raising effort at the YMCA in Port Talbot, West Glamorgan, non-stop between 29 September and 3 October 1980.

The ability of the human skin to tolerate heat and pain and emerge totally unscathed after being subjected to extremities of either has long baffled medical science. Intensive studies of native tribal rites, some of which involve the infliction of what would be, to ordinary people, unbearable atrocities, have, to date, failed to yield a positive answer as to why certain men and women seem to be impervious to pain of any kind.

A 19th century study of the Aissaoui tribe of Algeria revealed how members whipped themselves into an ecstatic frenzy through vigorous dancing and incessant chanting and wailing and, at what seemed to be the peak of their ecstasy, were able to run sharp-pointed and sometimes white hot irons into their heads, eyes, necks and breasts without pain or injury. It seems probably today that it was un unknowing use of a form of self-hypnosis, similar to that used by Indian fakirs, which rendered them insensible to ordinary feelings of the flesh. Another possibility may have been the use of naturally occurring narcotics in plants.

Self-inflicted disfigurements, seemingly created without pain were a custom of the North American Indian tribes right up to the early part of this century. The native Maoris of New Zealand were still practising 'human sculpture' on themselves less than a hundred years ago, decorating their skins with cruel tattoos by carving and gouging out their own flesh with sharp instruments. In India, the Brahmins would impale themselves on giant hooks and hang, suspended, without any visible show of pain. The infliction of a wide variety of seemingly barbaric injuries for penance is also practised by certain tribes. There is a 19th century account of a man from Northern India who, to serve his penance, sat for most of each day with his left arm held aloft, pressing the nails of his left hand tightly into his palm. After a considerable time the nails began growing into the palm where they became embedded so deeply that they were clearly visible poking out of the other side of his hand.

The tattooed head of a New Zealand chief

Rubber man

James Morris was the original India Rubber Man who starred in hundreds of Barnum and Bailey shows. The skin on his nose, chin, arms and legs was so elastic that he could pull it outwards an astonishing 18 inches from his body. When released, it simply twanged back into place like a rubber band. Morris could stretch the skin of his chin and neck so far that it covered his entire face!

Another form of freak skin endurance which has baffled doctors for centuries is the remarkable, inexplicable ability some people have shown to be able to withstand extreme temperatures and even fire itself. Human salamanders, men who could endure searingly hot ovens, were a great favourite of the freak show followers of the last century. A man called Chamouni, the celebrated Russian salamander, styled himself as 'The Incombustible'. His most spectacular feat was to enter an oven with a raw leg of mutton and remain inside until the meat was well cooked.

Eventually, the act ended in tragedy, when 'The Incombustible' was burned to death as he strived to endure ever-greater temperatures. His ashes were sent to his home town in Russian and a monument was erected over the spot where they were finally laid to rest. A Havana-born freak show favourite called Martinez became known as the 'French Salamander'. As an apprentice baker during his boyhood he had exposed himself to very high temperatures long before he joined the circus circuit. He once remained in an oven, which had been specially erected in the middle of the Gardens of Tivoli, with the temperature set at a scorching 338 degrees Fahrenheit for 14 minutes. His pulse when he entered was 76. On leaving the oven it was racing at 130. Yet, despite the obvious dangers attached to his favourite feat, it was one which Martinez performed on numerous occasions, often before huge crowds, with no seemingly ill-effects.

One well-documented account of human heat endurance, which appeared in the *Glasgow Medical Journal* of 1859, relates how a baker's daughter in the city remained in her father's oven for 12 minutes at a temperature of 274 degrees.

Among the most amazing fire worshippers who endured immense heat without appearing to be burned were the Navajo Indians of North America. One account from the end of the last century tells how before each ritual and fire-worshipping ceremony a gigantic pile of wood is set ablaze and left until flames are licking as high as 100 feet. Then a whistle is the signal for a dozen warriors to leap from the shadows, each one carrying a narrow pole topped with a ball of eagle down. At the height of the inferno, each warrior has to burn the down completely off the pole – a seemingly impossible task because of the intensity of the fire which sends sparks shooting onto the legs, arms and bodies of the participants.

The account of the Navajo ceremony says: 'The remarkable feats . . . are performed in a dance that follows.' A cacophonous blowing of horns heralds the entry into the fire ring of ten or more tribesmen, all of whom are carrying bundles of shredded cedar bark in each hand. The warriors run around the fire four times, before igniting their bundles. Then begins a wild race around the fire, the speed of running causing the bundles to send searing, shooting sparks across the arms and legs of the men who are carrying them. The object for each runner is to catch up with the man in front and rub the flaming bundle, as though it were a sponge, into his back. A warrior who is caught, says the eye-witness account 'in turn catches up with the man in front of him and bathes him in flame'. The account adds: 'From time to time, the dancers sponge their own backs with the flaming brands.' When a bundle is almost totally consumed by fire – and so rendered useless for the purpose of the dance – the man holding it drops it and retires from the fire arena. The smouldering wood he has left behind is then picked up by other Navajos who are watching the dance and they bathe their own arms and legs in the 'left-overs'. There is no record of any warrior ever having been injured at a fire dance. That fact truly amazed onlookers, for apart from a covering of earth which they ritually apply to their bodies, they have no other form of protection whatsoever.

Other amazing skin anomalies include the strange case of the man who sweated blood. He was an Italian officer, who in 1552, during the war between Charles V and Henry II of France, was told that he was under threat of being publicly executed. The man became so distraught and terrified for his life, that observers were astonished to see his skin react by sweating blood from every part of his body.

In a similar case, a young man from Florence, who was about to be put to death by Pope Sixtus V, became so horrified at the prospect that as well as sweating blood he also cried bloody tears. In 1869, in a small Belgian village, a most remarkable thing began to happen to 23-year-old Louise Lateau, whose life previously had been completely ordinary. One Friday afternoon, blood suddenly began to flow, for no accountable reason, from the left side of her chest. Every Friday after that, the same thing happened. And each time, on the day before, pink, oval shapes would appear on the poor girl's hands and feet.

Every week Louise would lose anything up to 1¾ pints of blood in the amazing 'stigmata' ritual. Doctors noted that during the period of blood-letting Louise seemed to be in a rapt and ecstatic condition. With similar cases of stigmata – a representation of Christ nailed to the cross – experts have only been able to offer as a reason the fact that religious fervour might lead to a hyper-excited or tense state which, somehow, causes the body to lose blood through the pores of the skin.

Rare cases of 'deciduous skin', or keratolysis, where humans actually shed their skins at regular intervals, have been recorded. A woman from Canterbury, New Zealand, who lived during the latter part of the 19th century, began shedding her skin at the age of 7 and continued to do so every few weeks for the rest of her life. According to medical records, the skin from every part of her body was shed, sometimes coming away in huge casts and sometimes simply sloughing off her body. It is claimed that the unbroken casts which came off her hands resembled a pair of gloves. Even the skin of her ears came off completely.

Cases of skin becoming as hard and wrinkled as tough animal hide are far more common. One extreme case was that of the 'Alligator Boy', a child who was exhibited by C. T. Taylor in Victorian England but whose identity has become obscured. Peep show visitors were invited to touch his skin, which really was as rough and leathery as that of an alligator, before recoiling in horror. It is not known what became of the boy.

One of the oddest skin disorders was observed by doctors in an unnamed 16-year-old laundress in the 19th century. Her face, neck, and the upper part of her chest had turned completely blue. The strange coloration, which could be rubbed off but would then return again, completely baffled the medical experts, for, apart from resembling an ice maiden, the girl was perfectly healthy.

The Amazing Prophecies of Old Mother Shipton

U rsula Southeil, born into the ignorance and cruelty of the Middle Ages, was hounded by her fellow men and women from birth because of her grotesque appearance.

Throughout her life, her unpitying neighbours kept up their demands for her death at the stake as a witch. She was possessed, they said, by demons and had been born a child of the devil. Against all odds, Ursula did, however, escape the unthinkable end which still befell so many hapless women accused of practicing the black arts in superstitious, sixteenth-century England. Justice prevailed; for she was, of course, no witch. Yet, she was, most certainly, cursed from the cradle to the grave.

Even today, in a more civilised world, her hideous deformities would more than likely evoke the same sense of revulsion which sent children scuttling away in terror and turned adults into hateful, suspicious enemies in those less-enlightened days.

Parish chroniclers recorded how Ursula Southeil's life of persecution reached its most wretched stage when she was in her early twenties. Undoubtedly, her appearance as a human freak was that of a caricature of the storybook witch. Her bowed, hunch-back did not stop her height reaching the giantess proportions of more than six-and-a-half feet; rolling layers of flab gave her an enormous weight of more than thirty stones; her huge, hooked nose was inches long; her pointed chin was covered with ugly, hairy warts. 'Her face,' wrote a priest, 'is frightful to look upon. And by virtue of her very grotesque appearance she is well suited to her part of the witch.'

Remarkably, the appalling deformities with which she was cursed did not deter Ursula from achieving fame of another kind ... as the most successful prophetess ever to live in England.

Dozens of predictions she made have come true with astonishing precision. She accurately foresaw the English Civil War, which broke out more than two centuries after her death, and pinpointed the exact date of the Great Fire of London as 1666 – a fact which posthumously earned her the fanatical following of the royal household of the time.

Records reveal that Ursula – or Mother Shipton, as she became known later in her life – also predicted the coming of the First and Second World Wars, the invention of the telephone, radio and television, the building of a railway system, cars and aeroplanes and the names of Kings and Queens who would rule hundreds of years after her death.

Her fantastic foresight is still revered by psychics the world over. But few can now spare a thought for the personal grief and misery she suffered during her own lifetime as a feared and despised human freak.

She was born in Knaresborough, Yorkshire, in 1488. Her mother was a beautiful woman called Agatha, who died while giving birth to the infant Ursula in a dark and miserable cave, where she had been forced to lived in utter squalor by simple-minded villagers. Agatha's crime, they claimed, was to have been raped by the village idiot. And the unbelievably cruel punishment they meted out was to banish her.

Agatha, apparently, died of shock as her baby entered the world. A sympathetic villager, who somewhat reluctantly had mustered enough pity to try to help during the birth, buried her close to the entrance of the cave.

Then, clutching the tiny figure of Ursula, she hurried back to her home.

From the beginning, Ursula was a bloated baby, with strangely distorted features. Her foster mother, whose name has become obscured by time, did her best to protect her, but as the weeks and months passed, Ursula grew more ugly and before she was a year old villagers had mockingly christened her 'Toad Face'.

Before long, folk-lore and myth began to attach to the unfortunate child a whole series of bizarre tales. Locals claimed that Ursula could summon evil, supernatural powers and was 'guarded' by a band of imps – ugly little men standing only two feet tall and dressed in red. Wild stories of sightings of Ursula's demonic guards abounded, fuelling the ill-feeling the entire village already felt towards her. Reports that the pathetic infant could levitate herself in her cradle also circulated.

As she entered her teens, Ursula became known locally as a witch. Her already gnarled, haggard and horrifically-ugly face, crooked gait and enormous bulk was soon inspiring such awe in local people that instead of staying away from her, they secretly began to consult her for advice on how to counter the curses of other witches and hex their enemies! Among themselves, however, they still condemned her as a witch – and demanded of the local magistrate that she be burnt at the stake.

Little is known of Ursula's personal view of her tragic predicament, other than the view expressed by the priest who wrote of her deformities but added, poignantly: 'Her understanding of her fellow's soul is most extraordinary.'

Perhaps it is the case that Ursula to some degree managed to turn her misfortune in some small way to her advantage. For, in her twenties, despite the continuing clamour for her death at the stake, two things happened.

Firstly, in 1512, at the age of twenty-four, she married a man called Toby Shipton. Where the man came from, or indeed why he should choose poor maligned and disfigured Ursula for a bride remained a mystery. What is known is that the couple were able to build a family which was large even by the standards of the time; Ursula gave birth to nine children, seven of whom survived her and all of whom were, mercifully, normal in appearance.

Secondly, she began to achieve recognition not just as a witch but also as a highly successful fortune-teller. Despite the sinister side of her reputation, clients began to flock to her from miles around. Her predictions of future events, as well as those concerning individuals, became legend and survived long after her death when, even today, Mother Shipton's prophecies carry great weight with thousands who have an interest in the foretelling of things to come.

According to parish records, old Mother Shipton did, once, appear before the magistrates of Knaresborough accused of being a witch. The charge was, however, dismissed, rather more likely through lack of evidence than the claim of a local woman called Peggy Fletcher that Mother Shipton frightened-off the justices with threats of spells and curses!

Latter-day seers insist that none of Mother Shipton's predictions have never proved false, although that assertion may be rather shaken by the old woman's prophecy that the world will come to an end in 1985!

But, although it is established that she lived out her final days in reasonably healthy old age, few could begin to guess today what torment she lived through, appearing to all the world as an atrociously disfigured witch, from the moment she was born into misery.

Daytime Prisoner

Truck driver Douglas Caplin was forced to quit his job and become a daytime prisoner in his own home ... because a freak allergy made his skin break out in weeping, red sores whenever he was exposed to sunlight. And doctors who were totally baffled by his condition also discovered that he was, for no apparent reason, suddenly allergic to cats, chrome, nylon, house dust, tar, detergents and penicillin. Even specialists said they could do nothing for him, and Douglas was forced to live in a twilight world of darkness, only able to mow his lawn and tend his garden by torchlight after nightfall.

Then, after seven years of misery, his brother Tony persuaded him to try acupuncture, the ancient Chinese needle treatment which is becoming widely used in Western medicine. For reasons as inexplicable as those which caused Douglas's sudden outbreak of bizarre allergies, it worked. And, early in July, 1982, Douglas emerged from his shuttered existence to feel the sunlight on his face once more.

'I've been born again,' said 54-year-old Douglas. 'I can now go out in strong sunlight with no problems at all. I've even got a new job lined up.' He added: 'I got so depressed by the illness that I almost felt like committing suicide.' I took only a month of acupuncture treatment at the Tyringham Naturapathic Clinic in Newport Pagnell, Buckinghamshire, to cure father-of-ten Douglas, whose wife Shirley used to have to dab a special cream to try to ease the pain on his delicate skin. 'Now the allergy has completely disappeared,' he happily declared, 'and I can't tell you what its like to lead a normal life again after everyone had given up hope.'

Horns, Tails and Noses

Horns, tails, nails and noses make up a truly oddball collection. But then, some of the World's Greatest Freaks are truly oddball characters.

Human horns, which have been known to grow to 11 inches long and 2½ inches in diameter, are far more common than is widely believed. Doctors in Mexico discovered a porter who hid a bizarre secret under his oddly-shaped red cap – no less than three horns sprouting at a lopsided angle from his forehead. In Paris in the 19th century, a woman identified only as the Widow Dimanche had a horn growing downwards from the dead centre of her forehead which was so long that it ended several inches below the level of her chin. Not surprisingly, to followers of the curious throughout the world she became known simply as 'Mother Horn'. In 1878, a Philadelphian doctor recorded the case of a sea captain who sported gnarled, horny growths from his nose, cheeks, forehead and lips. On several occasions, the 78-year-old mariner's horns appear simply to have dropped off, only for new ones to grow in their place.

In *Anomalies and Curiosities of Medicine,* Gould and Pyle report the case of a teenage girl, Annie Jackson, who lived in Waterford, Ireland, during the last century and grew hideously misshapen horns from her 'joints, arms, axillae, nipples, ears and forehead'. Modern studies have revealed that the growth of horns is far more likely to occur in women than men. Gould and Pyle also relate a case second-hand – which may be apocryphal – of a woman patient who had a scarcely believable 185 horns growing from her body.

Cases of congenital multi-horn growths on members of certain African tribes have been recorded, and legends of the lost Ju-Ju tribe of horned 'Devil Men' in Haiti remain today. However, serious doubt overshadows the so-called proof of their existence, which was the discovery of the remains of

Golden nose

Famous Danish astronomer Tycho Brae, after whom a huge Moon crater is now named, nosed his way into the world of freaks after his own nose was sliced off in a swordfight. Armed with bundles of money he had been given for research by the King of Denmark, he ordered surgeons to clamp on his face a brand new, specially designed one, made of solid gold. He wore it with shining pride till the day he died.

Central forehead

This picture was published in August, 1813, in a London magazine. The portrait was reputed to have been drawn in 1588 when the subject, Margaret Vergh Gryifith, was sixty years old. The horn, which was supposed to have been in the centre of her forehead, was four inches long.

Duck bill

Legendary Wild West lawman Wild Bill Hickock would hardly have inspired such fear as he did in bandits and gunslingers if his true nickname had ever leaked out. Close friends actually knew US Marshal James Butler Hickock as 'Duck Bill' because of his huge nose and freakish, protruding lower lip. After he was shot dead – ironically at Deadwood, South Dakota – on 2 August 1876, while holding a wild set of poker cards (aces and eights) the truth was finally revealed.

---

two shrunken, mummified figures with horns and hooves. The 'Devil' analogy was, however, certainly applied to horned men and women exploited throughout the world during the 19th century freak show boom.

Human tails are also not such a rarity as you might expect. Towards the end of the 19th century, a black child aged 8 weeks in Louisville began to grow a tail from the base of his spine which, within months, had grown to 2½ inches long with a base 1¼ inches in circumference. The tail, like that of a pig, was fleshy, with no sign of bone or cartilage running through it. As the boy – or 'Pig Boy' as he was cruelly dubbed – grew up, the tail seemed to cause him no problems whatsoever, so he kept it, despite the fact that even in those days doctors could probably quite easily have removed it.

In the early 1890s the most incredible tale of a tail emerged, when a travelling physician discovered a 12-year-old boy with a growth from the base of his spine which was an amazing 12 inches long. The youngster, from Cochin China, who became known as the 'Moi Boy' in medical circles, overnight became a world-famous oddity. Photographs of him appeared in the journal *Atlantic Monthly*. The 'Moi Boy's' tail, the longest ever recorded in a human being, was completely fleshy, without any trace of bone. Yet, just like an animal, he seemed to have perfect control over it.

Human noses, thanks in part nowadays to the party piece of the false nose, have become a vital part of the anatomy at least in cosmetic terms. Plastic surgeons now make a fortune out of performing 'nose jobs' on the rich and famous and even the deeply embarrassed yet less wealthy who have scrimped and saved in an effort to have their shame surgically removed or improved.

In the category of freak noses, there is really only one contender, 18th century Yorkshireman Thomas Wedders (or Wadhouse). His nose was 7½ inches long, and became the *objet d'art* on which dozens of contemporary illustrators focused their attentions. Graphic line drawings of simpleton – for that's what he was – Wedders and his nose still exist. Who knows what he could have achieved had he been born into the era of the freak show?

Romesh Sharma

Human nails can, of course, be grown to any length required – and Romesh Sharma, of Delhi, India has gone to great lengths to ensure that he has nailed a world record. From his picture, it's easy to see why: the curly, tusk-like nail on the thumb of his left hand would, if straightened out, measure an incredible 26½ inches.

Romesh set about getting himself into the record books from scratch. He was only 19 and still a student when his sister angrily told him that she was embarrassed to walk down the road with him because his finger nails were too long. Ashamed, Romesh scissored and filed away until his sister was happy. Back at college though, he found himself being chided once more, for giving in to her demands, and fellow students laid down the challenge: 'We bet you can't grow your nails long again.'

It was a challenge Romesh took up sharply. He agreed to let the nails on the fingers of his left-hand grow completely unchecked. Within four years that now-famous thumb had begun to curl itself in a perfect, if brittle, figure 'O'. In 1970, the curiosity with the crazy cuticles was beginning to receive such worldwide acclaim that he found himself the star exhibit in places as far away as Japan.

Shortly after appearing in the Land of the Rising Sun, where the distance from that moon-shaped crescent at the base of the nails to the very tip earned him a good sum, Romesh fell in love, and vowed to his young bride-to-be, as he had vowed to his sister, that he would cut his nails once more and forever keep them in trim.

This time, he broke his promise. Indeed, Mrs Sharma still waits today for the pledge to be honoured. At night in bed, her husband lies with his left arm dangling outside the sheets, lest he should roll over and crack the previous nails which have seen neither scissors, clippers nor file for 15 years. She helps bath him and buttons all his clothes for him – and she has long since grown

Tailed duke

The first Duke of Wellington, who as the Iron Duke became one of Britain's foremost statesmen and military leaders, could only ride on horseback using a specially adapted saddle with a hole at the rear to accommodate a small, bony, vestigial tail which grew from the base of his spine.

Romesh Sharma

used to total strangers knocking at the door of their home to catch a glimpse of his claws.

Romesh, his wife and two children have, indeed, become celebrities in Delhi – a mystical, magical place where it is not unusual for spiritual devotees to seek the ultimate perfection of putting the world at their fingertips. There is one cruel cut, however. A religious man from the same country has inched ahead of Romesh's pursuit of the record.

Mr Shridar Chillal, of Poona, has grown his five left hand nails to a total length of 108½ inches. The aggregate length of the nails on the left hand of Romesh – despite that record-breaking thumb – is just slightly less than 100 inches. Now Romesh has set himself a new challenge; to cut through that record by growing his nails even longer. And he says: 'This time, I've got the blessing of my wife – and I'm determined to nail a new record!'

Chapter Seven

Freaks of Life and Death

Human Fireballs

What bizarre freak phenomenon was shared by more than 200 people who suddenly burst into flames and died, engulfed in super-hot infernos which barely scathed the everyday objects around them? How have their bodies been reduced to ashes by searing temperatures of well over 2,000 degrees Fahrenheit, a staggering twenty times greater than the heat a normal person should be able to generate naturally?

The enigmatic question of spontaneous human combustion has baffled scientists for more than a century. Close studies into why ordinary folk – aged between four months and 114 years in documented cases – should, for no apparent reason, turn into human fireballs, have so far yielded no positive answers. While walking, driving, boating and even dancing, men and women have ignited and burned to death in front of terrified onlookers while everything around them, sometimes the very clothes they were dressed in, survived with scarcely a scorch mark.

Hundreds witnessed a woman erupt into flames on a dance floor at the Corn Exchange, Chelmsford, Essex, only seconds after happily swinging into a tango with her partner. In an instant, all that was left of her was cinders. Yet her party dress remained as crisp and fresh as it was when she had put it on.

On a freezing winter's day on 5 December 1966 in Coudersport, Pennsylvania, gas meter-reader Don Gosnell discovered one of the most startling recent cases of spontaneous human combustion when he entered the home of respected local doctor J. Irving Bentley. He found only half the good doctor's leg, and a three-feet wide hole on the floor on the spot where he had simply vanished in a blaze which claimed his body, yet left intact highly flammable rubber and plastic objects all around it. Gosnell raced from the house, yelling, somewhat understatedly, 'Dr Bentley is burned up!'

Incredibly, even the rubber tips of the walking frame used by the semi-invalid doctor had not been touched, less than a foot from the ashes of his body which had burned, according to forensic experts, with an intensity more than twice that of an ordinary house fire. Only inches away, paint on a bathtub had failed even to blister.

'It was,' said the local coroner, 'the oddest thing you've ever seen.' Yet the strange fate which befell Dr Bentley was far from unheard of.

The first written medical record of spontaneous human combustion occurs in a journal published in 1673, which cites the case of an unfortunate Parisian man who, after drinking heavily for three years, was reduced to a puff of smoke and a pile of ash while sleeping on a straw bed. Only part of his skull and a few finger bones remained intact, but the straw beneath him which should have been wiped out completely, remained. On 9 April 1744, the daughter of 60-year-old Grace Pett of Ipswich watched in horror as her mother swiftly sizzled before her 'like a log of wood consumed by a fire'. In this case also, Mrs Pett had been an alcoholic – adding substance to the theory that strong liquor drinkers and smokers were the most likely victims – and articles around her body which should have been destroyed, such as a silk screen and a pile of children's clothes, were untouched.

A little under a century later, in 1828, an eminent Canadian physician, Dr James Schofield, reported the case of an Ontario man seen 'standing erect in the middle of an extended, silver coloured blaze with the appearance of the wick of a burning candle.'

On 18 May 1957, Anna Martin was found burned to a crisp in a room in her home in West Philadelphia without a source of fire. A medical examiner estimated that to incinerate her so completely, a heat of 2,000°F would have been required. Yet the room was cold, with no fire. Her shoes remained intact. Twenty feet away, a pile of newspapers was not even singed.

In 1951, Dr Wilton Krogman encountered a case in St Petersburg, Florida which he calls 'The Improbable Case of The Cinder Woman'. And he adds: 'When I think of it even now, the short hairs of my neck bristle with fear'. A report in the American Science Digest takes up the story: 'When her son left Mary Hardy Reeser's small apartment on the evening of 1 July 1951, he saw a familiar sight: her 175-pound body comfortably ensconced in an over-stuffed chair, her slippered feet stretched out before her, and wearing a rayon-acetate nightgown. Less than 12 hours later, her apartment revealed what Krogman called "a scene macabre beyond words". In the stiflingly hot room, only some severely heat-eroded coils springs marked the remains of the chair.

'The ceiling and walls, above only a level of four feet, were covered with oily soot; 12 feet away from what little remained of the body, two candles had

---

Tune of cheer

An amazing man with a musical head became the toast of society partygoers in London and New York during the 1950s. Known only as Professor Cheer, the Russian-born American advertised himself as 'The Man With The Xylophone Skull', and could produce remarkably melodic tunes by hitting his head, in strict tempo, with two mallets.

melted. The nearby newspapers and the linen on the daybed only inches beyond were unsinged. There was no stench of burned tissue. All that remained of the 67-year-old widow were a few pieces of calcined vertebrae, a skull shrunk to the size of a baseball and a wholly untouched left foot.'

The expert Krogman could only say later: 'Only at three thousand degrees plus have I seen bone fuse, or melt so that it became volatile. Yet that's what happened to what remains of this victim's skeleton. The heat was more than twice that of the hottest conventional house fire. The apartment and everything in it should have been consumed. I simply cannot tell why the effect was so localized.

'How could 170 pounds of flesh burn without detectable or discernible smoke or odour permeating the entire building?'

In the 19th century doctors declared that all victims of spontaneous combustion were heavy drinkers, heavy smokers and quite elderly. Research has totally dismissed such a simple answer. Explanations for the freak phenomenon have included the assertion that bodies steeped in alcohol generate combustible gases which can react with deposits of fat. Excessive deposits of phosphorus in the body has also been put forward as a cause.

But medical science is as baffled today, despite intensive research, as it always has been, and the question of why so many men and women have inexplicably turned into human fireballs remains totally unanswered.

Amala and Kamala

Deep in the heart of India, the terrified and deeply superstitious villagers of Midnapore made an impassioned plea to the travelling missionary who had just arrived in their small community. They begged him to exorcise the evil spirit of a dreaded 'man ghost' and rid them forever of the nightmarish ghoul which seemed to stalk them like a wild, savage beast.

On 17 October 1920, the Reverend Joseph Singh, perhaps seeking only to allay the imagined fears of simple minds, agreed to lay their supposed phantom. With a posse of nervous villagers, he was led to a series of holes in a clearing, from where it was believed the mysterious spectre appeared. He

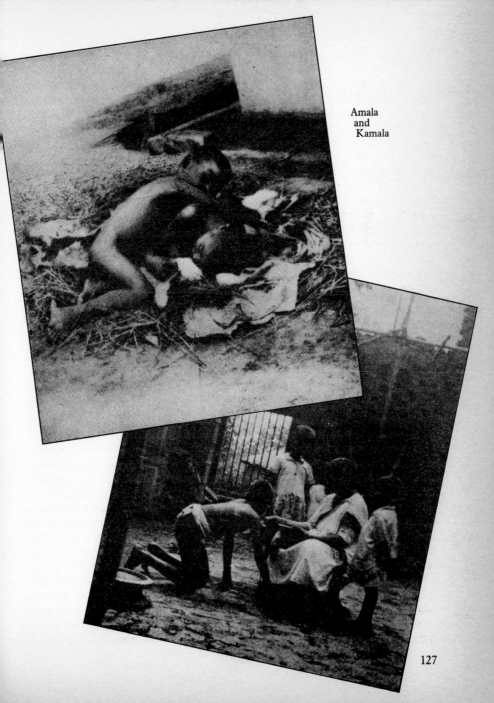

Amala
and
Kamala

waited there for several hours with the terrified villagers keeping their distance. The Reverend Singh's diary records what happened next:

'All of a sudden, a grown-up wolf came out from one of the holes. This animal was followed by another of the same size and kind. The second one was followed by a third, closely followed by two cubs ... one after the other. Close after the cubs came the ghost – hand, foot and body like a human being; but the head was a huge ball of something covering the shoulders and the upper portion of the bust, leaving only a sharp contour of the face visible, and it was human.

Close at its heels there came another awful creature like the first, but smaller in size. Their eyes were bright and piercing, unlike human eyes.'

What the Reverend Singh was describing, and what the fearful had thought to be a 'man ghost' was, in fact, two little girls who had been abandoned by their mother and raised from infancy by a she-wolf. The Reverend Singh was witnessing what still remains the only properly-documented case of feral children being brought up by an adopted animal mother.

As soon as the Wolf Girls of Midnapore had emerged, snarling and on all fours, from their cave, the entrance of which was almost camouflaged by a termite mound, the petrified villagers killed their she-wolf guardian. The youngsters themselves were rescued by the Reverend Singh, who managed eventually to take them to an orphanage, where he christened them Amala and Kamala.

The two little girls could run swiftly on all fours, but were unable to stand up. They ate only milk and raw meat, lapping and tearing with sharp teeth like the wolf cubs they had been raised with. They could not talk or laugh, yet their sense of smell was acutely developed, like the natural hunters their she-wolf mother had been teaching them to be.

Their exact ages could only be guessed at, but it was thought they were about seven years old when they were discovered. Their only gestures were those of wild animals and their sole reaction to the human society into which they were thrust was one of utter bewilderment. It was hardly surprising that Amala survived in captivity for only a year. When she died, her sister, ironically, displayed her first human emotion. Kamala cried two tears.

Slowly, Kamala began an almost imperceptible metamorphosis from wolf cub to human being. Eventually, she learned to stand upright, eat cooked food and speak a few words. By the time she died, nine years later, she had a vocabulary of 30 words. She was thought to have been about 16, but with the mental age of a three-year-old. Although she had been almost totally animal when found, her genetic adaptability had been quite remarkable. Little Kamala died a human being.

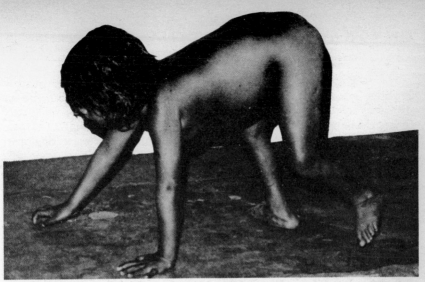

Tissa, brought up by monkeys in Sri Lanka

More Children of the Wild

Human freaks from the wild, like the Wolf Girls of Midnapore, have not only fired the imagination for centuries. They have sparked the seemingly never-ending search for man's lost elusive ancestor – the Missing Link. During the early 1880s, a much-exhibited female freak rocked the medical world, and, in fact, was widely accepted as the living proof of Darwin's theory.

Krao, a native of Indochina who shot to fame all over Europe, was indeed a bizarre, misshapen creature, appearing to be half-ape, half-human, with a thick covering of hair on her face and what appeared to be a mane running down the back of her neck. According to reports at the time, she displayed 'extraordinary prehensile powers of feet and lips' with the ability to pick up very delicately the most fragile objects with her toes and contort her mouth into amazing, monkey-like expressions.

One observer wrote: 'When annoyed, she throws herself to the ground, screams, kicks and gives vent to her anger by pulling her hair in a very peculiar way.' It seems, however, that Krao's rantings were more like those of a petulant, tantrum-throwing child than of a so-called 'Missing Link'. For she was, indeed, only seven years old when she was first exhibited as a peep show attraction.

Other claims to wild fame by human freaks have proved to be enormous, though entertaining, frauds in the mould of master showman and peep show trickster Phineas T. Barnum. For example, the Wild Men of Borneo, two

129

THE WORLD'S MOST FANTASTIC FREAKS

ferocious-looking and incredibly strong midget brothers who became a huge attraction across America, were neither wild nor from Borneo. They were christened Hiram and Barney Davis, though later changed their names, for the sake of their show, to Plutano and Waino. And, far from tearing apart unwary Western sailors who landed in their far-flung territory, they were apparently born in either Connecticut of Long Island.

Zip The Man Monkey, another freak exhibited by Barnum from the mid-19th to early 20th century, may have appeared to be a savage, neanderthal monster with his close-shaven head topped only by a hard, horny knoll of hair. But it is likely he was actively encouraged to grunt and act like a wild beast, rather than let anyone begin to guess that he might just be a simpleton, born to a poor Negro family in Brooklyn.

Such harmless, manufactured stories, designed to enhance the crowd-pulling potential of what, after all, really were human freaks, fail to detract from recently documented cases of wild men and boys.

In 1973, a youngster was found in the jungles of Sri Lanka who had apparently been adopted by a family of monkeys. When discovered, he was about ten years old. He could neither speak nor stand up. Yet, like the Wolf Girls of Midnapore half a century before, he was able to run swiftly on all fours and could use his hands and feet to cling and pick up objects with remarkable skill. Is he another example of the true feral child?

And as recently as May 1982, staff at a hospital in Kenya, East Africa, were shocked to find a new arrival scavenging for scraps in their backyard. The hairy, grunting being on all fours is slowly being 'tamed' by medical experts who reckon him to be aged about 20. They are convinced he is truly an example of that rare phenomenon, a human freak from the wild.

Many tales of genuine finds of true wolf-children must have brought the story of Romulus and Remus to life in the sensation-hungry 19th century. One of the strangest was reported in *Chambers' Journal*. It told how a boy in India was actually captured from a roaming pack of wolves with whom he seemed to be totally at ease; hence captured rather than rescued.

It was discovered that the child's parents had mysteriously 'lost' him while he was a babe-in-arms and there was a great village celebration when the family was re-united. Joy turned to horror, however, when the wolf-boy's mother and father tried to coax him back into the normal routines of any family home. He was found to be troublesome and virtually impossible to control – just like a caged wild beast, in fact.

Often during the night, the boy would wail and moan in a guttural, animal cry for hours and hours on end. When dusk had fallen, it became a nightmare time for his parents and brothers and sisters who had so eagerly opened their arms on his return. It is claimed that one moonlit night, the boy's feral screams attracted two wolf cubs who had been prowling near his home. He had been tied by the waist to a tree by superstitious villagers and his plaintive wails were thought only to have been cries of anguish at his predicament. However, by the light of the full moon villagers swore that they saw the two cubs gambolling around the tree trunk where the little boy was held captive. Uncannily, it was as if they all knew each other – and the cubs only departed as day was about to break.

According to the report, the wolf-boy did not survive long. He never spoke and never displayed any signs of human intelligence. In another case from around the same period, a boy who had allegedly lived with a wolf pack for six months after being snatched from his home by the she-wolf, only had one desire when he was at last found by his frantic mother: to return to the wild. He would growl and snarl if upset and would eat any scraps of food, especially meat which he would devour in an animal fashion, that was thrown to him. He could drink a full pitcher of milk in one single gulp, and refused to wear any clothes, even during the most bitter winter weather. He showed a great liking for bones and would gnaw at them with canine relish for hours. He could not speak a single word. He was ugly, filthy and was constantly trying to escape from the human world which he totally rejected.

In many cases of purported wolf-children, the youngsters were found to have hard, calloused layers of skin on their elbows and knees as a result of going around only on all fours. The *Zoologist* magazine of March 1888 related six such cases. In one, the boy concerned could only understand sign language, yet had an acutely developed sense of hearing.

Another curious account is that of two children in the orphanage of Sekandra, near Agra in India, who were discovered living among wolves. One was found by a trooper on a mission for a local native governor. He was passing alongside the bank of a river around noon when he was astonished to see a large female wolf leaving her lair followed by three cubs and an infant boy.

The boy scuttled along with his adopted 'family' of beasts on all fours – and when the trooper tried to catch him, he ran as fast as the cubs and was able to keep up easily with the she-wolf. The trooper returned to the nearest village to seek help to rescue the boy and a team of willing hands was recruited to dig the youngster out of the den into which he had so nimbly raced. Though still little more than a toddler, the boy struggled desperately to free himself when the rescue team snatched him from his 'home'.

As they forcibly carried him back to civilization, he lunged and tried to bolt for every hole or gully that was passed. Later, when he was confronted with adult people, he was petrified, but when he saw other children, he snarled at them ferociously, trying to attack and bite them. Back at the

131

orphanage, he totally rejected cooked meat but drooled at the sight of raw flesh and bones, hiding all his food under his hands the way a dog holds his paw over his meat.

The story behind the second so-called wild child at the orphanage in Sekandra is equally bizarre. The little boy in question this time was, it is claimed, carried away by a she-wolf in March 1843, after his Hindu mother had left him in a sheltered 'safe' spot near the rice field.

For a year, there was no sign of the child, and his heartbroken parents were forced eventually to give him up for dead. Suddenly, however, a wolf, followed by her litter of cubs and a strange, small ape-like creature were sighted about ten miles away from the village where their son had mysteriously vanished.

Villagers gave chase to the strange-looking creature and, on catching him after a breathless chase, recognized him from a small burn-mark on his knee to be the boy who had gone missing from beside the rice field. His elbows and knees had become hard and horny as a result of moving around on all fours. He would not eat anything apart from raw meat and could never be taught to speak. His only form of communication was a strange, muttering growl.

Despite being sent away from his real parents, the boy never even made an effort to adapt to a human way of life. In the winter of 1850, he made several unsuccessful attempts to escape and in the following spring he made it to freedom and the jungles of Bhangapore.

The Curse of Youth

His hair was white, his skin gnarled and wrinkled, and the varicose veins stuck out on his arms and legs. When he walked, his shoulders had the droop of a tired, aged man. He was so weak, he could barely talk. It came as no surprise to family, friends and neighbours when, inevitably, Charles Chesworth collapsed and died of old age. He was seven.

When he was born, to perfectly normal parents in a Staffordshire village, the baby had appeared to be perfectly healthy and ordinary, apart from minor imperfections in his shoulder and bottom jaw. But by the age of three, he began to develop with frightening speed. Within 12 months, he reached sexual maturity and began to grow a beard. Over the next three years, until his death on 14 March 1829, he withered away into old age and senility.

Gazelle boy

The Gazelle Boy, a supposedly feral child, was caught, with incredible difficulty, in 1967 running with a herd of wild gazelle in the Arabian desert. According to a letter to *John Bull* magazine, those most graceful animals had brought him up, and he could match their incredible bursts of speed on his two legs.

Doctors are still baffled by the rare, startling disorder which causes young children – even newborn infants – rapidly to develop the characteristics of adults and sometimes die of old age at a time when they should normally just be reaching puberty. Little boys, some as young as 2 or 3, have been known to grow beards, speak in deep voices, feel sexual desires and exhibit the body hair of men.

Girls have sometimes had the physical characteristics of women at an even younger age – as early as 6 months. They menstruate, grow breasts and, by the time they should simply be toddlers, are capable of bearing children of their own. They are victims of precocious development, a disease caused by a massive imbalance of hormones in the body.

In recent years, doctors throughout the world have been forced to stand helplessly by while the devastating disease speeds up the ageing process of its little victims, often resulting in death after only a few years. In one case, a little girl became a feeble, arthritic, bedridden old woman while her parents watched in horror. New hormone treatments are being tested in places such as the US Government's National Institute of Child Health and Human Development. But the disease itself has been recorded as far back as the days of Ancient Rome.

Brewster's Journal of 1829, recording the case of Charles Chesworth, says: 'At the age of 6, he was 4 feet 2 inches tall and weighed 74 pounds. In all respects, he was as well developed as any adult'. Louis Beran, born on 29 September 1869 at Saint-Gervais, France, was so tall, strong and mature at the age of 6 that he shunned other children and, according to a local physician, 'helped his parents in their labours, doing the work of a man'.

Nineteenth-century dime museums across America put on show a 'Man-Boy' who, at the age of 15 months, weighed almost 7 stones and displayed all the signs of maturity of a youth many years older. The 'Man-Boy', who was said to have been a phenomenal size at birth, died after only a few years – years which had turned him into a hideous old man – on Coney Island. At about the same time, the French physician Desbois recorded the case of

---

Dental display

Polish strong man Siegmund Breitbart gave a dazzling display of dental power on 27 November 1923, when, using only a bit between his teeth, he controlled the reigns of a team of horses pulling a wagon containing 50 people through the streets of Washington DC. Breitbart said he performed the incredible stunt to draw publicity to his circus show, which had just rolled into town!

Tattoo you

Britain's most decorated man is Wilfred Hardy, of Huthwaite,
Nottinghamshire, who has covered an eye-catching 96 per cent of his body
with tattoos and has now started on his cheeks, tongue, gums and eyebrows.
The most tattooed lady is Mrs Rusty Skuse of Aldershot whose husband,
who always had designs on her, has covered 85 per cent of her in patterns.

---

another 'Man-Boy', aged 11, who, during one period of his kaleidoscopically
fast maturing process, shot up an astonishing 6 inches in 15 days.

The Victorian tome *Anomalies and Curiosities of Medicine* describes 'a boy
of four years and three months who was 3 feet 10½ inches tall and weighed 54
pounds'. His face was like that of an adult and his sex organs were fully
developed. However, mentally he was dull, quite obstinate and self-willed.
He was not different to other children until he was three after which his voice
began to break and his sexual organs developed. Another medical publication
tells of a boy born at Willingham, near Cambridge, in 1741, who showed
signs of puberty at the age of 12 months. When he died four years later, he
had the appearance of an old, senile man.

Exceptionally precise measurements were made during a close study of
young Philip Howarth, who was born at Quebec Mews, Portman Square,
London on 21 February 1806. Within a year, he had lost his babyish
roundness and become awkward as his limbs began to grow like those of a
boy much older. Before he was 3, his sex organs developed and his voice
broke.

At the age of 3, he was 3 feet 4½ inches tall and weighed 51¼ pounds. His
thigh measured 13½ inches round, his waist 24 inches and his biceps 7
inches. He was reported to be 'clever, very strong and muscular,' despite
being terribly ugly as a result of the disease that seemed to be racing him
through life. By all accounts, however, the ageing Howarth did survive at
least into early adulthood.

After dozens of similar cases over the centuries, many of which have ended
so tragically, doctors in America are now experimenting with a synthetic
hormone which they believe may succeed in arresting precocious development. A team at Massachusetts General Hospital, led by Dr Gordon B.
Cutler Jr, is working on the drug, which is thought to be able to block
production of sex hormones. It is hoped to be able to use it on children, who
would undergo a course of the drug before it was withdrawn at the
appropriate time to allow puberty to occur normally.

A Ripe Old Age

If it is the curse of youth to die prematurely of old age, then it must be a blessing of life for those who do live to a real ripe old age. Longevity is something almost everyone hopes to attain, whether we like to admit it openly or not.

Quite remarkable claims to old age litter the history books, many of which seem unlikely. The bounds of credulity were stretched to absurd limits even as recently as 5 May 1933, when a news bureau quite solemnly released a story to the world, with a Peking dateline, about the death of Li Chung-yun who was purported to be the oldest man on earth. The agency claimed that he was no less than 256 years old when he died, having been born in 1680 which really is very difficult to believe!

Genuine error, deception and even outright fraud symbolise many of the claims of super centenarians of the past. Freak show exhibitors of such alleged characters almost always added the first number that came into their heads onto the true age of their wrinkled and gnarled showpieces.

Celebrated centenarians of the past have been discovered not to be just one person at all, but the sum total of years of a father and son who shared the same Christian name. It is only comparatively recently that official censuses throughout the world have begun to properly chronicle birth certificates to establish true ages.

The greatest properly authenticated age to which a human has lived is, at the time of writing, 116. Shigechiyo Izumi, who lives on a Japanese island 820 miles south-west of Tokyo, was born there on 29 June 1865 and was recorded as a 6 year old in his country's first official census in 1871. Today, he watches television and advises that the best way to lead a long life is, simply, 'not to worry!'

The oldest authenticated centenarian in Britain, which currently has a population of around 4,000 hundred year olds, was Miss Alice Stevenson, who died in 1973 with the distinction of being the only Briton ever to have birth and death certificates 112 years apart.

One of the most baffling recent cases, far removed from the clear-cut issue of Miss Stevenson, was that of Charlie Smith of Barlow, Florida who, in 1955 managed to obtain a social security card after claiming to have been born on 4 July 1842.

Smith said he had grown up as a child in Liberia and had no documentary proof of his birth. His card was issued, however, with the US Department of Health, Education and Welfare adamantly refusing to disclose their sources of information about his age. Smith, fully accredited, was thus able to claim to be celebrating his 137th birthday on 4 July 1979, just three months before his death. It was only quite recently that county records in Florida turned up a marriage licence for him from 1910, showing his age to be 35 then. After exhaustive research, it was finally decided that he died roughly two months short of being a true 100 years old.

Perhaps the centenarian feat which was against more odds than any other was that achieved by identical twins Eli and John Phipps, born on 14 February 1803 in Affington, Virginia, who both lived to be more than 108 years old. The chances of that happening again are calculated at an astonishing 700 million to one. The oldest twins in Britain have been Robert and Mary Beau, who celebrated their 100th birthday on 19 October 1973. Mary, now Mrs Simpson, lives in Etton, Cambridgeshire. Robert died before the end of 1973. The oldest triplets ever to live on record were Faith, Hope and Charity Caughlin of Marlboro, Massachusetts, who were born on 27 March 1868 and all lived for at least 93 years.

In many cases, claims to fantastic longevity seem all the more spurious nowadays in the light of investigations in Sweden, which is the only country in the world to officially investigate the death of every claimed centenarian. So far, the Swedish Government has not verified one single case of anyone living over the age of 110. Longevity claims for entire races or creeds, such as the Brahmin priests of India or the ancient Greeks and Chinese are steeped in myth, folklore and mystery, with not a scrap of evidence that such occurrences are scientifically possible.

There are, however, suggestions that a Yorkshireman named Henry Jenkins just might have lived to the fantastic age of 169 which was, on his death in 1670, widely enough believed to earn him a place in history. Chancery registers were said to have 'proved' that he had appeared in court, sworn an oath and given evidence in a trial 140 years before he died. There is a further record which reveals that he appeared in court again to give evidence at the age of 157. In old age, Jenkins is said to have been able to recall the Battle of Flodden Field of 1513, which was fought when he was barely 12 years old. It is also claimed that he was in such good health that even after he passed his 100th birthday he was able to swim against the strong current of a fast-flowing stream.

Another celebrated English super-centenarian was Thomas Parr who later became known as 'Old Parr'. He was a poor farmer's servant who was born in 1483. He is reported to have lived to the grand (possibly grandiose) old age of 152. And, although he was a batchelor until he was 80, he certainly seems to have lived life to the full and made up for lost time after that. For, shortly after he became an octogenarian, he took his first wife, who lived, as his wife for 32 years before she died. Eight years later, at the age of 120, untiring Thomas took the plunge again and re-married.

It is claimed that old Thomas lived not only an extraordinary marital life, but was also an indefatigable labourer, toiling ox-like in the fields until he was 130, at which age he was said to still be able to thresh with quite dazzling speed. News of his incredible life reached London, and it is said that a succession of noblemen who visited his humble abode finally persuaded him to visit the capital for an audience with the King.

It was that journey, or rather the excitement of it, which is thought to have hastened Thomas's death. Huge crowds had gathered to greet him as the carriage in which he travelled pulled up at the gates of the palace. In the royal court, the King and all his acolytes were reported to have been amazed by his intelligence, speed of thought and dexterity. Within a year of his rise to stardom, however, old Thomas was dead.

A surgeon who examined his body found that all his organs were in a perfect state; his bones had not even ossified as is usual in the extremely aged. The surgeon could not find the slightest cause of death, and so finally decided that the high life killed him. His impression was that good treatment and being over-fed in London had caused his demise.

A monument in Westminster Abbey today still marks the memory of old Thomas Parr, whose great-grandson, it is claimed, emulated his celebrated forbear's centenarian stand and lived to the age of 103 in Ireland, where he died during the 19th century.

Nature is the great natural re-cycler of our world. And perhaps that's what accounts for the amazing case of a German magistrate, who died in 1791 reputedly aged 120, who really got his teeth stuck into life. In 1787, after spending years of difficulty trying to chew his food in a toothless mouth, he was astonished to discover that, at the age of 117, eight new teeth had begun to grow. Delighted with his new set, his happiness turned to sorrow when, six months later, they all fell out. Within days, however, yet another new set of eight teeth began to grow in their place ... and the long since retired old legal eagle lived out the rest of his days with a happy, toothsome grin!

Another hale and hearty super-centenarian was Anthony Senish, a farmer in Limoges who died in 1770 aged 111. According to reports, he toiled in his fields right up to his demise and still had the strength and determination of a carthorse. Considering the frailty which usually accompanies old age, it was his quite incredible boast that he had never shed a drop of blood or touched a drop of medicine in his entire life. He still had a full head of hair and excellent vision. He attributed his longevity to his staple diet of chestnuts and corn.

Which naturally raises the question asked all the time of centenarians today: Just how do you keep young and beautiful at such a ripe old age? It is a question which has prompted some entirely unexpected and very surprising answers.

An Englishman called William Riddell who is said, although there is no precise verification, to have lived to 116, swore all his life by the bottle. He adamantly refused to ever touch a drop of water, quenching his thirst instead with brandy. Every day he quaffed a tot of varying size and was convinced that the booze kept him bounding along in good health. Thomas Wishart of Annandale, Dumfries, who died in 1760 aged 124 said he had chewed tobacco every day of his life since he was 7 years old. He explained that his father had introduced him to the weed at such a tender age to suppress his hunger while he was shepherding the animals alone for hours on end in the mountains.

John de la Somet of Virginia, who lived until 1766, actually smoked himself to death ... for an alleged 130 years! He claimed that inhaling smoke worked wonders for his system and agreed perfectly with his constitution. In fact, he insisted, the more he smoked the better he felt. The British Medical Journal recorded the case of a physician called Dr. Boisy from Havre who lived to be 103. He was still doing his daily rounds until his death and lauded the medicinal effects of both alcohol and tobacco, being a smoker and imbiber himself of no mean standing. Another centenarian surgeon who lived around the same time found his elixir of life in the port bottle, which he uncorked and half-drained daily.

Another 'grand old man of medicine', Dr R. Baynes of Rockland, Maine, believed that quite the reverse was true. A strict teetotaler, he even condemned the drinking of tea! He lived on a strict vegetarian diet until his death at around the turn of the century, aged well over 100, drinking only water, milk or occasionally chocolate and banishing even potatoes from his frugal diet.

Apart from his rigid dietary habits, Dr Baynes harboured another theory for his longevity – the avoidance of beds! He refused to sleep on a bed, or even a mattress on the floor from the age of 50, preferring instead a less comfortable slumber on a reclining iron chair, over which he spread a few blankets for warmth.

There are many instances of centenarians surviving on incredibly frugal fare. Scotland abounds with stories of the over 100's who have lived on porridge alone.

In Germany, a labourer called Stender who toiled in the Holstein region until his death in 1792 at the age of 103, was said to have survived in the latter stages of his life entirely on oatmeal and buttermilk. The virile Baron Baravicino de Capelis, who married four times, his last wife bearing eight children, became the oldest man in the Austrian Tyrol in the eighteenth century on a completely meat-free diet of eggs, tea and sweet cordial which sufficed him until he died aged 104.

The Zombie Girl

In 1936, a ragged, wretched woman was found wandering aimlessly, as though in a trance, around the roads skirting a modest farm. She appeared to have totally lost the power of speech and she cringed fearfully under a tattered cloth she was carrying if anyone approached.

When she was taken to hospital for care and treatment, she prompted this incredible description from an American photographer: 'The sight was dreadful. That blank face with the dead eyes. The eyelids were white all around the eyes as if they had been burned with acid. There was nothing you could say to her or get from her except by looking at her, and the sight of this wreckage was too much to endure for long.'

The poor, inhuman woman was finally identified as Felicia Felix-Mentor. The farm around which she had been found roaming was that of her brother. But how she came to be there, and in such a bizarre state, was a mystery. For medical records revealed that Felicia Felix-Mentor had died of a sudden illness and had been buried twenty-nine years previously.

Her strange case, documented and photographed by the American Zora Hurston, has baffled the world everywhere apart from anyone who knew, was related to or, indeed, lived in the same country as Felicia Felix-Mentor. To the people of Haiti there has always been a simple, spine-chilling answer to why this freak-woman seemingly rose from the dead.

They say she was a zombie. One of the walking dead brought back to enslaved life by Voodoo, the bizarre and fabled religion of which horror films are made but which still, today, is a feared belief of, astoundingly, more than 90 per cent of the Haitian population.

Successive tyrants 'Papa Doc' and now 'Baby Doc' Duvalier have surrounded themselves with a fierce private army known as the *tontons macoute*; a *tonton macoute* being a travelling voodoo magician. Beneath the hocus-pocus, however, lies more than a show of strength and a convenient means of suppression of superstitious subjects.

In his book *The Invisibles*, British anthropologist Francis Huxley tells of a so-called zombie who was seen in his own village in 1959. In a state of shock, apparently, the zombie was taken to a police station, where local officers would have nothing to do with him. In the street, a stranger gave him a glass of salt water and he then managed to stammer his name. His aunt, who lived nearby, positively identified him. According to her, he had died and been buried four years previously.

Haiti has bred other, less reliably-documented accounts which seek to

A Haitian Zombie ceremony

explain appearances of wildly staring, automaton-like human freaks; supposedly raised from the dead by bokors, or voodoo sorcerers, who claim to weave evil spells over corpses, turning them into mindless, re-born slaves.

Another, latter-day description of an alleged encounter with a zombie, by a man called William Seabrook, makes blood-curdling reading: 'The eyes were the worst. It was not my imagination. They were in truth like the eyes of a dead man, not blind, but staring, unfocused, unseeing. The whole face, for that matter, was bad enough. It was vacant, as if there was nothing behind it. It seemed not only expressionless, but incapable of expression. I had seen so much previously in Haiti that was outside ordinary, normal experience that for the flash of a second I had a sickening almost panicky lapse in which I thought, or rather felt, "Great God, maybe this stuff is really true ..." '

What would seem, to any outsider, to be superstitious mumjo-jumbo, is treated with deadly seriousness by the bokors and their disciples in the former French slave colony that is Haiti today.

But what really did happen to Felicia Felix-Mentor and others like her? Could she – and so many more – simply have been people buried alive after being drugged into a death-like, catatonic trance and then recovered from their graves to be seen later, wandering aimlessly around, ghoulish, freak aberrations of human beings?

Perhaps relevantly, Article 246 of the Old Haitian Criminal Code states: 'Also to be termed intention to kill is the use of substances whereby a person is not killed, but reduced to a state of lethargy, more or less prolonged, and this without regard to the manner in which the substances were used or what was their later result. If following the state of lethargy the person is buried, then the attempt will be termed murder.'

In the case of Felicia Felix-Mentor, 'more or less prolonged' was, or might have been, 29 years. Is that really what could have turned her into a freak from an unimaginable nightmare ... a zombie girl?

Six Year Fast

In a shuttered room a frail teenage girl wakes, stirring only slightly between crisp, white sheets. In the street outside, the new day's visitors have already arrived and wait, patiently and silently, to be called to her bedside.

One by one, or occasionally in small family groups, they are eventually ushered from daylight into the still-dark room. Slowly, as if to conserve every possible ounce of energy, the girl raises her head to observe, as she has done many thousands of times, the latest pilgrims who hail her as a saint.

Since Christmas 1975, the worshippers, the miracle-seekers and the simply curious have been flocking to the tiny Portuguese town of Tropeca, where 18-year-old Maria Vierira, her face a deathly-white mask, lies awaiting the audiences with her humble followers. Since Christmas 1975, Maria has apparently neither eaten nor taken a single drink of water.

Her incredible fast has been verified by completely mystified medical experts, who say she should have died within a month. Yet the fragile girl, who is not only defying all laws of nature but is also claimed to have immense healing powers, explains her survival by saying that she saw a holy vision. 'I talked to Jesus and the Holy Mother,' she says. 'They told me to help the poor people. They said I didn't have to eat any more, so I don't. They said they would provide and that I should have faith.'

Faith has drawn busloads of pilgrims from all over Portugal to the modest home where Maria lives with her parents, entombed always in her darkened, shrine-like bedroom. At first, her family were outraged by her refusal to take any form of sustenance. Says her mother, Elena: 'We even sat by her room for days trying to catch her sneaking food – but we never did.' Now her parents believe she has been blessed by God. Like priests and doctors who have closely examined and scrutinized her, they can find no logical, earthly reason why she should still be alive. One specialist from Oporto, who has verified Maria's total lack of intake of food or water, discovered that her average weekly urine output is a mere 50 cubic centimetres, or only 5 per cent of the average 1,000 cubic centimetres of a normal human.

In the face of such medical evidence, however, at least one priest in Tropeca disbelieves Maria's startling condition and claims. Father Enrice Joso says: 'She looks like an epileptic and I think the trances she has are epileptic fits.' More sinisterly, he adds: 'I think her mother has taken her to witches.' This alarming verdict is not, though, shared by Father Joseph Mauel, from nearby Oporto. He insists: 'From a human point of view anything is possible on a spiritual level.' Indeed, time and again, cynics have been confounded by the skeletal form of little Maria, who always maintains that her fast is on holy ordinance to save the world's sinners.

Her neighbours in Tropeca have been amazed by her fantastic healing powers. One, Evelina Menezes, recently told a North American newspaper: 'I have seen her heal people . . . lots of them. I saw one man carrying a child who could not walk. They went into Maria's room, and when they came out the child was walking.' Another neighbour spoke of the hordes of pilgrims 'who come to be blessed by our saint . . . some even crawling on their knees.'

Maria's mother tells how her daughter goes into a trance when she is healing: 'Her face becomes just like Christ's Her eyes are surrounded by dark circles and there is a crown of thorns on her head. Her face gives off a glow.'

Thousands of pilgrims have claimed to have witnessed a strange radiance being emitted from Maria's body and many attest to her seemingly divine ability to heal even the supposedly incurably sick.

No food

Doctors were completely baffled by the case of a 19-year-old girl, who became known as the 'Market Harborough Fasting Girl' after the name of her home town. She supposedly ate literally nothing between April 1874 and December 1877, when she died after surviving only on occasional doses of morphine, with neither food nor drink passing her lips.

Of her own destiny, the fragile waif of a teenager who is herself a medical miracle, has remained silent. Christmas 1981 marked the sixth year of her fast and, though she certainly grows no stronger, she is far from immobile. Her movements are slow, for her strength is slight, yet she remains totally articulate and determined to continue what she believes is her divine mission. Meanwhile, pilgrims still descend in their thousands and despite the fact that by now, had they willingly handed over money, Maria could have moved to far more opulent surroundings, she has refused to accept a single payment and remains in her rather austere family home guided by her religious vision. For she says she has no need of food or water, or other worldly things.

Young Mothers

On 13 July 1982, a girl of 10 was recovering in hospital after giving birth to a 4 pound 8 ounce baby. Both were said to be 'quite satisfactory.'

The unnamed girl was taken to hospital in Houston, Texas on a special flight from a country town in the east of the state for the delivery, which doctors had predicted would be premature. Immediately after the birth, cagey staff at the Hermann Hospital refused to say whether the infant was a boy or a girl or – honouring a request of total secrecy by the girl's guardian – give any other details.

The case is far from being unique, however. The world's youngest-ever mother was Linda Medina, a peasant's daughter from the Peruvian Andes, who was flown to Chicago for hospital treatment in 1940 when she was six years old, and her baby son was aged 15 months. Linda suffered from the disease which can kill youngsters from 'old age' by speeding up their ageing process to a phenomenal rate.

She was sent to America to be treated by Dr Karl John Karnaky. How she became a mother at such an incredibly early age remained a mystery to specialists. Her superstitious parents could only offer Indian folklore reasons; her mother Donna Loza said she had been bitten by a snake with curious powers over women and her father said that she had bathed in an enchanted mountain lake known as the 'pool of birth'.

As the photograph here shows, 9-year-old Venesia Xoagus was feeling well

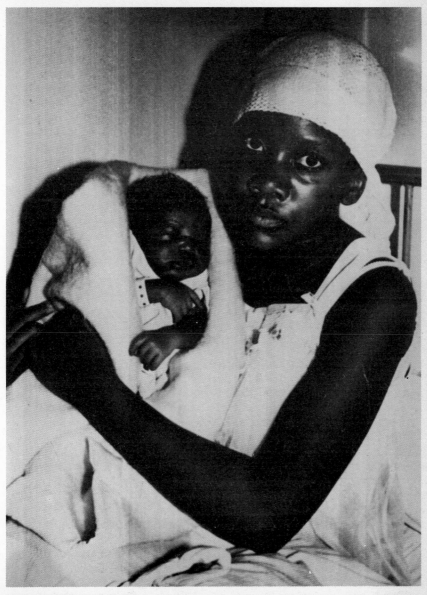

Nine-year-old Venesia Xoagus

enough barely a week after giving birth to a baby boy at Otjiwaronjo Hospital in Southern Africa, to pose with the infant. In July 1980 she became the youngest mother ever to give birth in that entire continent.

The oldest mother on record is Mrs Ruth Alice Kistler, born at Wakefield, Massachusetts on 11 June 1899, who gave birth to a daughter, Susan, at Glendale, near Los Angeles, California on 18 October 1956, when she was 57 years and 129 days old. In Britain, Mrs Winifred Wilson, of Eccles, Greater Manchester, had her tenth child, a daughter she christened Shirley, when she was 55 years and 3 days old on 14 November 1936.

There is an unauthenticated report that a septuagenarian gave birth in the Welsh town of Clwyd on 15 May 1776, in her 46th year of marriage. But, it is claimed, the baby boy who would have been 72-year-old Mrs Ellen Ellis's 13th child, was stillborn.

A Man Becomes a Mum

Young soldier Nochmen Tenenbaum served with great distinction in the Polish Army, earning bravery medals for rescuing several people from drowning and earning promotion to sergeant. But, after he was demobbed at the age of 24, he discovered that something quite startling was happening to him. He found himself gradually changing into a woman. A year later, in 1936, doctors and nurses at a Warsaw clinic were astonished when Tenenbaum, still wearing his men's clothes, asked to book a private room – because he was pregnant. He was admitted and, shortly afterwards, gave birth to a healthy, bouncing, 9-pound baby. The amazing incident is believed to have been the first time that a person who has changed sex has become a mother.

Other startling sex changes were happening in Britain at around the same time when two sets of sisters became brothers within four years of each other. Marjory and Daisy Ferrow grew up as girls in the seaside town of Great Yarmouth, Norfolk. But when they were 13, according to newspaper reports: 'they both developed characteristics that made them hold aloof from other schoolchildren, and eventually forced them to sacrifice scholarships which they had won to Yarmouth High School for Girls.'

The family left town for a few years. And when they returned in August

Man gives birth

'Man Gives Birth' is a headline editors throughout the world would love to put in their newspapers. It has, in a manner of speaking, already happened. On a number of occasions, males have been born with the foetus of a twin in their own bodies. In one famous case in Mexico City a huge tumour on a baby boy's back was opened, to reveal a crying, perfectly healthy infant.

1939, Marjory had become pipe-smoking Mark Ferrow and Daisy had become David. It was believed at the time to be the first instance of two members of the same family changing sex. Then, in 1943, a tragedy brought a similar case to light.

Mary Weston lived with her sister Hilda at Oreston, near Plymouth. She was a superb athlete and a key member of Britain's Olympic team, having been women's national champion javelin thrower in 1927 and having won an international shot-putting title in 1934. Two years later, she became a man and changed her name to Mark. In 1937, Mark married Alberta Bray, a 20-year-old blonde who had been a girl friend, first of Mary and then, of course, of Mark, for years.

Hilda's life also changed, but with no such happy ending. Operations at Charing Cross Hospital were suggested when she tried to register for national service in one of the armed forces and, though she changed her name to Harry, depression after the operations proved unbearable. Harry hanged himself from a tree, aged just 26.

Ronnie Rigsbee was born a boy at Durham, North Carolina, in 1944. But by the age of 6, he had begun to realize that he was very different from his playmates. 'I always associated with girls,' he recalled later. 'I couldn't understand why . . . but I just felt that I should be a girl.' After he joined the US Navy at the age of 17, Ronnie was comforted and told that his disturbed feelings were just 'a passing phase'. It was a phase that stayed with him, however. For in 1970, when he was 26, a leading New York doctor began a series of operations which eventually turned Ronnie Rigsbee into Susan Janette Fontaine.

She took a job as a barmaid, but quickly discovered that she had swapped one set of problems for another. She was raped, which added to her turmoil and mental anguish, and tried to commit suicide several times. After one attempt, a sympathetic nurse befriended Susan and took her to church. 'I realized I had made a terrible mistake,' she said, 'if God had made me male when I was born, then He intended me to be male.'

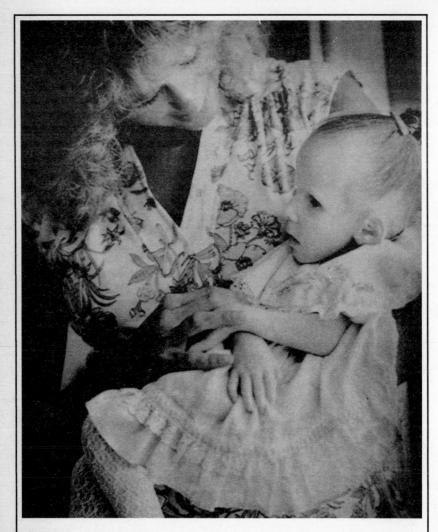

Dying of old age

This five-year-old little girl, who weighs only nine pounds, suffers from the rare and tragic disorder which speeds up the ageing process. As yet, there is little that doctors can do to help sufferers.

In November 1980, Susan's breasts were surgically removed, and Ronnie Rigsbee emerged from hospital to become a croupier at a Las Vegas casino. Through years of unease and confusion, he now says that he is finally completely happy to stay the way he is. He knows he will never be able to have a normal sex life, but he says: 'I feel it is loving and caring that are important. I am finally at peace ... I have found myself at last.'

Sex changes, or, rather, stories about them, may seem well suited to some of the more salacious newspapers. But it is worth recounting that they began to attract intense medical interest more than a century ago. One of the best documented cases is that of Catherine/Charles Hoffman, who changed sex in 1870 at the age of 46. Catherine/Charles had lived with a male lover for 20 years, before marrying a woman. It is highly likely that Catherine/Charles was a true hermaphrodite – a double-sexed human. Hermaphrodites were extremely rare, highly-prized oddities in Victorian times, drawing the attention of leading doctors and freak experts all over the world. It is extremely doubtful whether any were actually exhibited in public, other than perhaps at the sort of underground 'fringe shows' which sometimes sprang up in an area overnight before moving on to evade the ever-following arm of the law.

One story of a true hermaphrodite, which bears repeating as an illustration of the mental anguish which must torture so many human freaks, is that of Marie-Madeleine Lefort, who checked into the Hôtel-Dieu, a public hospital in Paris, as an old man aged 65 suffering from chronic pleurisy. He was bald and had a long, flowing beard. In terrible health, he moaned to hospital staff of having led a miserable existence, barely scraping a living.

It was only when an autopsy was performed two months later, after the old man died, that hospital staff realized the full extent of the misery he had been through. They discovered him to be the same person who had been examined by an eminent panel of doctors at the age of 19, as a girl. His condition as a hermaphrodite had totally confused him and he had told the hospital staff that though he had only had the feelings of a man for 16 years, he was puzzled about why he had been taken for a girl when young. He was, of course, both!

Chapter Eight

Freaks of Size and Strength

General Tom Thumb

Never even from the legendary land of Lilliput could have come a figure quite so amazing as Charles Sherwood Stratton. He was a most rare human being; not dwarf, but a true midget – a perfectly proportioned person in miniature. He real name may sound unfamiliar, but the baby who was born on 4 January 1838, lager achieved worldwide fame as the most celebrated freak who ever lived – General Tom Thumb.

He became the jewel in Barnum and Bailey's collection of human oddities, the darling of the Palace of Queen Victoria and three-quarters of the way towards being a millionaire. In a blaze of publicity, he married a midget woman and, in moments of great pomp and pride, became a close confidante of the Duke of Wellington.

Stratton had been a normal enough – even strapping – infant, weighing in as he did at birth at 9 pounds. But, remarkably, he remained at exactly the same weight until he was 5 years old. His height at that age was a diminutive 2 feet 1 inch. With such a medical marvel on their hands, his parents did what to them and to hundreds of other mothers and fathers in the early part of the 19th century was a perfectly natural thing to do. They put their little boy on public exhibition.

News of the amazing midget's shows in Bridgeport, Connecticut, travelled far and wide until it fell upon the ears of Phineas T. Barnum's half-brother Philo. The master showman reacted like greased lightning; within hours he tracked down the little fellow and signed him on the spot to work for three dollars a week.

With his usual passion for overkill and hype, Barnum re-christened the tiny toddler 'General Tom Thumb' and billed him as a 'dwarf of eleven years of age, just arrived from England'. Barnum was determined that his prize capture should be taught to enrapture audiences by being 'autocratic, impudent and regal', and set about schooling him day and night in the wacky ways of the peep show world.

General Tom Thumb's first public appearance was marked by his strident, almost pompous recitation of one of Barnum's pun-ridden monologues. The little midget portrayed himself as an arrogant, barking bombast – and the public loved every second. He was coached in a variety of garishly-costumed roles by Barnum, including Cupid, Napoleon, Yankee Doodle Dandy and a semi-naked gladiator, and the paying punters couldn't get enough of it.

As word of the thumbnail-sized General's performances spread, people flocked from miles for the privilege of attending his shows. He quickly

Mr and Mrs Tom Thumb

established himself as Barnum's most inspired acquisition and indeed became something of an ambassador for the great showman. Literally overnight, he became the talk of New York and, less than a year later, the toast of London during an incredibly successful tour in England. A delighted Queen Victoria, who stood barely 4 feet 11 inches tall herself, summoned him to give three Royal Command Performances at Buckingham Palace, where he soon earned the nickname 'Pet of The Palace'. The Queen is said to have been most definitely amused by the little manikin's strutting and strange antics.

General Tom also became a good friend of the Duke of Wellington, who was another great fan of his. It is claimed that during one Palace performance in which he was playing Napoleon, the Duke asked him what he was thinking about. 'Sir,' he replied, 'I was thinking of the loss of the Battle of Waterloo!'

For every show, Barnum always billed General Tom as being six years older than he actually was. Advertised as 30½ inches and 18 years old, he was in fact, only 12. By maturity, his height had reached its miniscule peak of 3 feet 4 inches. In adulthood, he was a singing, dancing story-teller extraordinaire. Decked in splendid costumes and with a neatly-trimmed, military-style set of whiskers, he became a little living legend.

When Tom decided to marry a midget woman, Lavinia Warren, who was almost exactly the same size as himself, Barnum decreed that the wedding was to be a razzle-dazzle showbiz affair with photographs, publicity and as much hullaballoo as it was possible to muster. It was a staggering success. Photographs of the half-pint-sized bridal couple together with their midget attendants were among the best-selling items in the early days of the camera.

General Tom and his bride settled down to make their fortune together, and at the height of their success, the much-loved midget couple had amassed a nest-egg topping three-quarters of a million dollars. They seemed destined to hit that magical million figure until Tom fell ill and, tragically, died of apoplexy in his home town of Bridgeport, Connecticut, at the age of 45. The little man went to his grave in the sure knowledge that he had conquered the world from the proud height of 3 feet 4 inches.

Dwarf race

One of the most astonishing races of dwarf people, who existed in the French Pyrenees for three centuries until the 1900s, was a clan called the Cagots, who were widely believed to have been the descendants of the inhabitants of a leper colony. One late 19th century medical report said 'They never exceeded 51½ inches in height, and had short, ill-formed legs, great bellies, small eyes, flat noses and pale, unwholesome complexions'.

Other Midgets and Dwarfs

The smallest human being who ever lived was Pauline Musters, a little midget girl from Holland who was exhibited as 'Princess Pauline'. The fragile creature, who weighed a mere 9 pounds at her heaviest, was 12 inches long when she was born at Ossendrecht on 26 February 1876. She never grew beyond 23½ inches tall and her vital statistics were 47-48-43 . . . centimetres! Her exact dimensions were recorded despite the fact that, as ever, her peep show bosses advertised her as being only 19 inches tall. Sadly, she became an alcoholic and, with a drink-weakened heart and also suffering from pneumonia and meningitis, she died at the age of 19 in New York on 1 March 1895.

Despite the fact that Lilliputian-sized freaks tend, like giants to lead shorter than average lives, there are records of two centenarian dwarfs – one of whom is still alive. Parish registers reveal that a woman called Anne Clowes from Derbyshire died in 1784 at the grand old age of 103. At her death she was only 3 feet 9 inches tall and a paperweight 48 pounds.

Susanna Bokoyni, a retired, Hungarian-born circus performer, celebrated her 103rd birthday at her home in Newton, New Jersey on 6 April 1982. She is just 3 feet 4 inches tall, and weighs a meagre 37 pounds. When she was born, way back in 1879, Susanna's father was confidently told by doctors that her chances of surviving were desperately thin. Yet she has proved the grim diagnosis utterly wrong. Sixty-seven of her incredibly active years were spent as a dancer. She performed all over Europe and eventually America as 'Princess Susanna' and became a noted circus and vaudeville artiste. During her travels, she became fluent in several languages other than her native Hungarian. She remains to this day in perfectly good health. Until she underwent a cataract operation as recently as 1978, she had never spent a day in hospital since the time a group of ashen-faced doctors peered into her cot and gravely shook their heads a century previously.

Entire races of miniature people have been discovered, the most famous being pygmy tribes such as the Obongos and Dongos of Central Africa, which has proved a rich hunting ground for freak-seekers with an adventurous thirst for the bizarre. Such tribes, which still thrive today in the dense bush of countries such as Zaire, often have many members of only between 3 and 4 feet high. Yet explorers beware: even the evil tyrant of Uganda, Idi Amin, was reluctant to venture too far into the domain of the men and women whose unerring accuracy with the poison dart is renowned as the shortness of their stature.

Count Josef Boruwlaski with his wife Isalina and their baby

In the latter part of the 19th century, an expedition to discover 'lost tribes' of wild-men dwarfs ventured deep into the jungles of Central America. In a previously unexplored region near the Isthmus of Tehuantepec, anthropologists found their elusive quarry and succeeded in bringing back to civilization – and the freak show – two Cotta tribesmen, midgets standing only 3 feet 6 inches tall.

Despite the success of such largely thrill-seeking missions, however, the *Guinness Book of Records* today states that the smallest documented tribe are the Mbuti pygmies who live near the Ituri river in Zaire. Proper records of the tribe reveal that the average height for men is 4 feet 6 inches and, for women, 4 feet 5 inches.

One of the most remarkable dwarf stories is presented in *Anomalies and Curiosities of Medicine* by Gould and Pyle. The eminent surgeons recount the tale of Geoffrey Hudson, the most celebrated English dwarf, who was born at Oakham in 1619. He was presented to Henrietta Marie, wife of Charles I, in a pie at the age of 8. He became her favourite pet freak and until his youth, he was said to be not more than 18 inches high. In his youth he fought many duels, one with a turkey cock. He was a popular and charming courtier, and proved his bravey and allegiance to his sovereign by accepting command of a Royalist company.

He once challenged a gentleman by the name of Croft to fight a duel, and shot his adversary in the chest after being ridiculed about his diminutive size.

Hudson himself met a nasty end. He was accused of being part of the Papist Plot and eventually imprisoned in the Gate House at Westminster. His enemies in politics had won. He died in prison in 1682 at the advanced age of 63.

Little Estelle Ridley was a midget who happily took one of the few forms of employment that was open to her, and became a figure of fun in a circus. Then, in the early 1870s, she devised an even better way of cashing in on her misfortune. Using cunning make-up and child's clothes, she was able to transform herself from a hard-living, foul-speaking 40-year-old woman into a pretty, innocent-looking 'little girl' called Fanchon Moncare.

With an accomplice called Ada Danforth, she regularly cruised between France and New York on ocean liners. Ada would explain to enchanted fellow passengers that Fanchon was an orphan whose parents had died in a fire. She would inherit a fortune and vast estates on her 18th birthday, but meanwhile she was in Ada's charge.

Fanchon would curtsey sweetly and skip off happily, clutching a china doll. And, at the end of each trip, she would dance gaily through customs still cradling the cherished doll, while Ada took care of the luggage. No-one ever dreamed of stopping the 'young child'.

Lilliputian inferno

There seemed nothing particularly sensational in the news item which ran in the New York press on 28 May 1911, about how 300 inhabitants of an entire village on Coney Island had, although unharmed, been made homeless by a fire which completely razed their small community, apart from the fact that all 300 were professional dwarfs and midgets and the village, which had been custom-built to suit their stature, was called, in fine movie style, Lilliputia!

But once the couple were in a hansom cab outside the dock, the sweet smile would fade to be replaced by a mask of evil. For in New York's bustling Chinatown, elderly Wing To waited eagerly, with a greedy leer creasing his wrinkled face. When the travellers arrived, the head of the doll was unscrewed and out poured a fortune in gems, stolen during their months in Europe.

The lucrative charade was only ended when Estelle, alias little Fanchon, fell out with an acquaintance over the affections of a professional New York gambler. Her rival in love went to the police in a rage, and a reception committee was waiting when the doll next arrived at the city dock. The midget was jailed for life, and later hung herself in her prison cell. Ada Danforth, the accomplice who was 10 years younger than the bogus 'little girl' in her charge, was sentenced to serve 20 years for acting as an accessory.

Lilliputian adults have, in the past, posed as babes-in-arms for rather more noble reasons. A dwarf named Richeborg passed unchecked to and from Paris during the French Revolution disguised as an infant in a nurse's arms. His were spying missions, for he had memorized and carried in his head top secret dispatches which were considered too valuable or too dangerous to be written down. Richeborg, who stood only 23 inches high, was never once suspected of being anything other than a tiny child. He died in Paris in 1858, aged 90.

Throughout history, dwarfs have not only been the court jesters, but also the close and trusted confidantes of kings and queens. Peter the Great of Russia, whose passion for the bizarre and often utterly distasteful included keeping the head of an unfaithful mistress pickled in a jar by his bedside to serve as a warning to her successors, also delighted in keeping a troupe of dwarfs for his amusement and entertainment. He was so delighted with his assembly of little people that in 1710, he threw a massive banquet for the marriage of his favourite, a male dwarf named Valakoff, to the female dwarf of Princess Prescovy Theodorovna. Later, dwarf marriages were banned in Russia because of supposed difficulties which might follow during childbirth.

Two dwarfs who did marry and build a huge family were Robert Skinner, who stood, at 25 inches, an inch shorter than his wife Judith. They had no less than 14 children, all of whom were perfectly normal, healthy, and eventually grew up to normal heights. Another popular theory which was current during Victorian times was that dwarfs were naturally more intelligent than people of normal stature. In 1868, a detailed post mortem examination was carried out on a dwarf who had lived to the age of 61 and was said to have been especially wise. Indeed, the examination did demonstrate that the weight of the dwarf's brain was one-nineteenth that of his body, whereas in a person of ordinary stature the ratio would be anything between one-thirtieth and one-fortieth.

Finally there was a troupe of dwarfs actually called 'The Lilliputians'. They performed throughout America in the late 19th century with great distinction as burlesque entertainers. The dwarfs, thought to have been gathered in Austria and Germany, were so good that they cost, apparently, a small fortune to hire!

Trumpet player

Matthew Buchinger was born in 1674. Although his flipperlike hands and feet were attached directly to his torso he could juggle, play the trumpet and bagpipes, and was reputed to be able to dance the Hornpipe. He was also married four times and fathered eleven children.

The Mighty Atom

Pint-sized Jorge Monteiro has earned the nickname 'The Mighty Atom' from cellmates at the Linho jail in Lisbon, Portugal, who are amazed as the little man's exploits – or, rather, 'sexploits' as newspapers all over the world have preferred to call them.

For although he stands only just over four feet tall and is something of a physical rake, Jorge managed to make love to 38 women while still behind bars! The diminutive Don Juan accomplished his incredible love trysts by simply squeezing through a wafer-thin gap in a dividing wall between the men's and women's sections of the prison.

Jorge was in jail in the first place for seducing 70 women and stealing their money in the time-honoured traditions of a deceiving Casanova. But he managed to escape after just four months – and then the story of his amazing prison love-ins began to emerge. Eventually, the elusive little man was recaptured, but even after a new trial in April, 1982, with Jorge on his way back to his cell, a Portuguese government official was forced to admit: 'He is just incredible. There is no way to stop him – even when we lock him up.'

During his second trial, Jorge had even had the impudence to brag to the judge of his adventures while incarcerated. 'What I did may have been wrong,' he did confess, 'but you have got to admit that it certainly was daring!' Prison officials who are baffled as to how any man could have got through the hole in the wall through which their miniature inmate seemed so easily to squeeze, decided after his latest trial that the only place for him was solitary confinement.

But a rueful jail official was forced to say: 'We can't keep him there for any length of time if he is behaving himself. Heaven only knows what he'll get up to again when we let him out. He's irrepressible. Women seem to adore him and for a man of such limited stature, he seems to be able to pack an awful lot of energy into that little frame.'

Meanwhile, some of the women he so cruelly deceived while at liberty have actually formed a fan club for him. And, while he may be known as the Mighty Atom inside the jail, outside his adoring followers call him 'Captain Rody'. That was one of the aliases the 40-year-old ultra-short super-lover used while posing as an army captain, an engineer and an insurance broker. One attractive 24-year-old divorcee fought back her tears as she told reporters: 'Let them say what they like about my Jorge, but to me he was always a perfect gentleman. His size is of no importance to me whatsoever. I will wait for him till he comes out of prison and fly to his arms – if he will have me.'

There was a rather nasty side to the pint-sized stud's passionate crime wave, however. Apart from seducing his doting victims before making off with money or jewellery he 'borrowed' from them, he also blackmailed those unwilling to part with their valuables with Polaroid photographs of their lovemaking. He was only caught after a number of them complained to the police. But even some of the women he most wickedly duped still hold the Might Atom close to their hearts.

One, from Lisbon, sighed: 'He is my little pocket dynamo and I shall always remember him. He was the perfect partner, always caring and always pandering to my every need, no matter how small. His size makes no difference at all. In fact, it makes him rather more endearing. I know that the things he has done are bad, but how could anybody feel angry at someone who is so sweet and adorable?'

With the flames of such unrequited love still burning so strongly for him, it seems unlikely he will ever abandon his favourite hobby. Even during his second trial, his female lawyer was forced to quit the case – because the Mighty Atom made a pass at her! It was a defence which, of course, in the end failed.

The little Portugese folk hero received a jail sentence of 7½ years from the judge, who was totally unimpressed by his heartless hanky-panky.

Yet another of his 'victims' insisted, though:'He is a legend and there will be lots of pretty girls like me waiting for him when he is eventually released. Jorge is just a little misguided, that's all. He really is one of the most gentle people I know and he would never, ever do or say anything hurtful to anyone.'

Four others had sat silently sobbing as the smiling, impeccably-dressed Mighty Atom stood in court while the full weight of justice was meted out to him: they were his wife and three children. 'I am happily married and have wonderful children,' he says. 'And I love them all . . . '

The Mighty Atom will obviously be greatly missed.

Kids' heroes

These men created the stories and the dreams on which children for centuries to come will thrive. The endurance of their works is unquestionable. Yet the legendary Aesop, whose Fables are beloved the world over, was a dwarf. And Hans Christian Andersen, the Danish genius of fairy tales, was a human skeleton, so thin that he stuffed his shirt with paper before ever appearing in public. He was dyslexic too, and so dictated his stories to be inked by another, unknown, hand.

The King of Giants

Walking tall ... that was Robert Pershing Wadlow, all-time King of the Giants. He towered head and shoulders above the freaks of which shows like Barnum and Bailey's were really made. From Goliath to the Fantasy Ogre at the top of Jack's beanstalk, giants and giantesses have fired public imagination as have no other examples of human hyperbole, alive or dead.

Wadlow remains the tallest accurately-measured man who ever lived. At the age of 22 when he died, he was a skyscraping 8 feet 11 inches tall – and still growing! When he was born in 1918 in Alton, Illinois, his mother and father, Addie and Harold, could have had no idea that the average-sized 8½ pound infant would rocket upwards in such an incredible way.

Up to the age of 2, his development was quite normal. Then, after a routine operation, and for no apparent reason, he began to grow abnormally fast. At the age of 5, he had a long way to look down on his kindergarten playmates from his lofty 5 feet 4 inches. Three years later, he was a six-footer. By 11, the tape measure was stretched to 6 feet 7 inches and just after he had started high school, at 13, his head was really in the clouds at 7 feet 1¾ inches. And he just kept growing and growing ...

When he was only 9, he could carry his father Harold, who was by then the Mayor of Alton, up the stairs of the family home and down again with ease. But then, Mr Wadlow senior was, to his son, a diminutive 5 feet 11 inches tall!

Wadlow was half an inch over the inevitable eight-foot mark shortly before his 17th birthday. A keen sportsman, he was an invaluable asset to his school basketball team as he was able to shoot down into the basket each time he had the ball for a certain score. For his incredible height he was, however, never obese. By the time he was 22, shortly before his death, he tipped the scales at a little over 31 stones. But for a man who was little more than half an inch from being nine feet tall, he carried the weight extremely well, looking, if anything, slightly thin!

It was Dr C. M. Charles, Associate Professor of Anatomy at Washington University's School of Medicine in St Louis, Missouri, who helped keep regular, scientifically documented records of Wadlow's progress towards the heavens. He was assisted by Dr Cyril MacBryde, who actually measured Wadlow's final recorded height just 18 days before his death on 15 July 1940.

Wadlow had suffered from a badly infected right leg, which was aggravated by a poorly-fitting brace. Ironically, he died just a month before

Robert Pershing Wadlow

the discovery of penicillin – the one thing that could have saved him. Quite surprisingly for the tallest man who ever lived, Wadlow never once succumbed to the lucrative offers from peep show bosses which poured in. It is hardly surprising that they were so desperate to get their hands on him, for it was the usual practice of rogues such as Barnum and Bailey to exaggerate wildly the height of their giants on display in an effort to prise yet more money from audiences.

Wadlow preferred instead to lead a quiet life with his parents, brothers and sisters, all of whom were normal sized, and shunned public life save for occasional newspaper photographs on special occasions such as his 21st birthday, when he was pictured amid the relatives he dwarfed. Indeed, he is reported to have looked an extremely dignified figure; a bespectacled man with the look of a scholar. He was sartorially elegant too, being exceptionally fastidious about his smart, specially-made suits and shirts.

After he died, he was laid to rest in an enormous coffin, 10 feet 9 inches long and 32 inches wide. Ironically, half a dozen accurate models of him were made shortly before his death by the famous artist James Butler. Where in life he had turned his back on the gaudy glare of the peep show, those models today still tour the world stored in huge coffins which have to be loaded through the freight ports of aircraft.

One of the models stood for a time in the main street of Helsinki, Finland, where it caused huge traffic jams as people stopped to stare at the world's tallest man, if only in the form of an effigy!

More Giants and Giantesses

The tallest man ever to live in Great Britain was Irishman Patrick Cotter O'Brien (1760–1806), who measured an incredible 8 feet 1 inch. His skeleton today stands preserved at the Royal College of Surgeons in London, where its height was re-checked as recently as 1975. How it comes to be there is the result of a remarkable story.

Throughout his life in Bristol, where he eventually settled, O'Brien lived in morbid fear of a cunning surgeon called John Hunter, who became obsessed with the idea of getting his hands on the giant's skeleton when he died. Hunter openly pursued O'Brien, threatening that he would 'boil him in a large iron pot till the flesh came off his bones' unless he agreed to the request. O'Brien, who staunchly refused to give the surgeon permission to have his body when he expired, often complained of being 'hounded to death' and begged the medical man to leave him alone.

The giant was, indeed, tormented all his life by the surgeon's vow to have his body, and by the spies he sent out to report on his movements. At the age of 45, O'Brien found his health deteriorating rapidly and, knowing he was on his deathbed, paid a group of fishermen to take his body after he expired and sink it in the middle of the Irish Channel, with heavy weights attached.

His dying wish to evade the clutches of the surgeon was not granted. Hunter, who had already bribed every undertaker in the city to hand over O'Brien's cadaver, managed to find the fishermen through his spies and out-bribed them too. O'Brien's body did, eventually, land in Hunter's giant melting pot, where all its flesh was boiled off to leave the surgeon – and, centuries later, the Royal College of Surgeons – in possession of the unwilling giant's skeleton. That melting pot that O'Brien had lived in such fear of has, ironically, been preserved as a museum piece too.

In recent history, America has towered over the world as the country which produces the tallest giants. Of the nine men positively known to have stood at over eight feet tall, the five tallest have all come from the United States. That figure includes the world's tallest living man, Don Koehler, who measures 8 feet 2 inches. Don, from Chicago, is the son of tall parents. He was born, with a twin sister who now stands at a rather more average 5 feet 9 inches tall, in Montana in 1925.

Perhaps the most famous super-tall freak of the peep shows was the Chinaman Chang Yu Sing, who was known to the discerning voyeurs of Victorian England as the aristocrat of giants. Chang, who was never accurately measures but was believed to have stood almost eight feet high, was known to have a passion for gold, jewels and pearls. He also had a penchant for the very finest clothes, and would refuse to appear on stage unless he was suitably dressed in embroidered silk, red velvet or panther-skin.

It was a golden rule among peep show bosses that, as well as being encouraged to exaggerate about their height, giants and giantesses had in their contracts a stipulation that they were never to be properly measured. So most reports of tall people who went on exhibit must, at best, be held to be rather questionable. For example, the costumes of circus giantess Ella Ewing always included an extra-large headress, and she was advertised at various heights up to 8 feet 4½ inches. She was scientifically measured at the age of 23, when she stood at 7 feet 4½ inches, though it is believed likely that she attained a height of about 7 feet 6 inches before her death. Ella became

The Chinese giant, Chang, with his wife and attendant dwarf

famous as the 'Missouri Giantess' when, at the age of 21, she joined the Barnum and Bailey circus and toured all over America, appearing also for a short time with Buffalo Bill's Wild West Show.

Ella, who became as well known for her warm, affectionate nature as she did for her height, had had a normal childhood until the age of about 10, when suddenly she began to shoot up, much to her embarrassment. Her parents, who were poor farmers, tried hard to shield her from stares and jibes, but after only a short while she was forced to quit school to escape the cruel taunts of her classmates. Ella turned to local fairs and shows to earn a living, but never really achieved great success until she was signed up by Phineas T. Barnum. With the King of the Freak Shows, the Queen of Giantesses made a fortune and was able to provide enough money to help her parents, who loyally followed her wherever she toured.

Ella was also able to buy herself a 120-acre ranch near her home town of Gorin, Missouri. On the land, she built a huge house, specially adapted to her gargantuan needs, with 15-foot ceilings, 10-foot doors and 7-foot windows. All the furniture was likewise proportioned and she was able at last to live in a home where she never had to stoop or feel uncomfortable. She was known as a kind, witty woman, who entertained with a wealth of stories about her experiences on the peep show circuit, and was a much respected member of the community until her death, at the age of 40, in 1913.

Ella's dying wish was that she should be cremated, so that her bones would never fall into the hands of vandals or even surgeons. Her father, however, could not bear the thought of it – so he arranged for her to be buried inside a solid steel casket in a cement-filled grave, over which he placed a guard for several years so that, in death, the 'Missouri Giantess' could have the privacy she so desired.

The world's tallest living woman is 18-year-old Zeng Jinlian (pronounced San Chung Lin) who lives with her parents and brother in Yujiang village in the Bright Moon Community, Hunan Province, central China.

At the age of 16, she was accurately reported to be an astonishing 7 feet 10½ inches, but is now said to have easily topped the 8 foot mark and continues to grow!

Zeng started springing upwards at the tender age of four months. She was the same height as her mother – 5 feet 1½ inches – before she was 4, and by her 13th birthday was 7 feet 1½ inches of little girl! Her hands measure 10 inches, her feet 14 inches, and her last recorded weight was 23 stones 2 pounds. Zeng suffers from acromegaly, a disease which has caused so many giants and giantesses to die while relatively young, and she already tires so easily that she can only go out walking with the aid of her family, who struggle to support her enormous body.

THE WORLD'S MOST FANTASTIC FREAKS

The tallest ever Englishwoman, who was also an acromegalic, was Jane Bunford, who was born on 26 July 1895 at Bartley Green, Northfield, West Midlands. Her growth rate was perfectly normal until the age of 11, when she started mysteriously putting on feet and inches at a phenomenal rate after receiving a head injury. At 13, she looked down on her parents from the awesome height of 6 feet 6 inches. Because of the disease which bowed and bent her spine, she measured a 'mere' 7 feet 7 inches on her death, at the age of 26, on 1 April 1922. Had her back not been so crippled and curved, it is estimated that her true height would have been 7 feet 11 inches.

What happens when a giant meets a giantess and two hearts begin to flutter . . . ?

It ended in marriage when Captain Martin van Buren Bates and Miss Anna Swan fell for each other. He was a towering 7 feet 2½ inches and she was actually three inches taller! The happy couple, who had travelled from America to England in a freak show, were wed at St Martin's-in-the-Fields on 17 June 1871.

They had already become immensely popular with Victorian England's keenest connoisseur of oddities, Queen Victoria herself, and the monarch was so delighted with them that she sent the bride a large ring and the groom an enormous watch as wedding presents.

After a huge wedding reception, which was attended by the Prince of Wales, and a tour of Scotland, they returned to the United States, where they made a fortune from freak shows before retiring to Ohio and a tailor-made home with 14-foot high ceilings and 8½-foot doors. One of their very first visitors was the midget Lavinia Stratton, then widow of the world-famous midget General Tom Thumb!

One of the most amazing dinner dates was widely reported in America in 1975, when 7 feet 2 inches tall giant Dan Gerber of Illinois called to escort 7 feet 5 inches tall giantess Sandy Allen of Shelbyville, Indiana.

Despite the close attentions of newspaper photographers anxious to record their soirée for posterity, the couple were determined that their date should be as normal as possible. After a visit to a local bowling alley, they set out for a restaurant where they discussed how much they enjoyed each other's company and how much they would both like to date again.

It's a bit rough on a young bachelor's wallet, though, when between them, he and his date manage to polish off 5 shrimp cocktails, 6 fillet steaks, a mountain of baked potatoes, two basketfuls of hot rolls, popcorn served in giant salad bowls and, for dessert, double helpings each of the following: ice-cream cake, pie and ice cream and banana splits!

If giant and giantess can be ideal partners, then so can a couple where, by dint of height alone, one partner really has to look down on the other! That's

Anna Swann's marriage to
Captain Martin van Buren Bates

Anna Swan with Admiral Dot, the smallest
man in the world at that time

169

the case with Mr and Mrs Max Palmer of Illinois, who represent the most extreme difference in the respective heights of a married couple.

At the time of their wedding Max stood a towering 7 feet 8 inches tall, while his bride Betty must have been sure she was entering into wedlock with a man she could look up to from her 4 feet 11 inches height, in high heels! Even with that little support there was an incredible gap of 2 feet 9 inches from the top of her head to the top of his. When another giant American, Henry Mullins, fell in love and popped the question, it was to a lady who stood 5 feet 3 inches tall to his 7 feet 6¾ inches, making a gap between them of more than 2 feet 3 inches. The couple met, according to Henry, when his bride-to-be went shopping in downtown Chicago, saw a sign saying 'Giant Sale' and decided to get one for herself!

Henry, who became a great music hall star, had changed his surname to Hite before launching out on a career which eventually spanned more than 30 years, so when he married he and his wife of course became Mr and Mrs Hite. Apart from his great sense of humour (and love of tall stories) Henry displayed remarkably nimble talents for a man of his height.

He was able to perform a quick-fire string of somersaults with the agility of an Olympic gymnast and he was a delightful tap-dancer in shoes which were more than 16 inches long. Despite his slender, well-proportioned frame, he was also something of a strong man, easily able to lift two men – one on each muscular forearm – and carry them around.

After he retired from the music hall, he became a travelling sales promoter for a meat packaging firm called Wilson's where fame followed him and he became known as 'Wilson's Giant'. He motored around in a specially customized car which had the front seat removed to make room for his incredibly long legs, enabling him to become his own back-seat driver!

Britain's tallest living man at present is 38-year-old Christopher Paul Greener who is a heady 7 feet 6¼ inches tall. Another Briton, Terence Keenan, is only a quarter-of-an-inch shorter, but, unhappily, he is unable even to stand upright. His growth rate was perfectly normal up to the age of 17, when he stood 5 feet 4 inches tall, but after that he began to shoot up skywards suddenly and abnormally.

Possibly the tallest giant who ever actually went on exhibition as a freak was a man named Machnov, billed as the 'Russian Giant', who drew enormous crowds in Victorian England. It is claimed that he attained the almost unbelievable height of 9 feet 4¼ inches, and indeed is also said to have had that height properly verified by medical experts, and not improperly exaggerated by circus masters and peep show bosses as happened in more than a few cases where the taller the giant was, the more certainty there was of a good day's takings.

Plenty of Pa

Jan Van Albert, one of the tallest men in the world, is pictured with his wife, who is five feet 7 inches tall, and their daughter.

Another much-displayed giant of the same era was Hugo, who was born in the Alpes-Maritimes and first appeared on show at the Paris Exhibition. At the tender age of 6, he was well over 4 feet tall, at 15 he had topped the six-foot mark by a clear 6 inches and, by the time he was measured at 7 feet 6 inches at the age of 22, he was still growing at the rate of roughly an inch every year.

Hugo had enormous bulk to go with his height, weighing-in at more than 31 stones. He completly dwarfed his parents; his father was only 5 feet 4½ inches tall, his mother 5 feet 6 inches, and it is not hard to understand why he needed a mammoth bed, 10 feet long and 5 feet wide, to ensure that he got a comfortable night's sleep.

Fantastic Fatties

Luke McMasters sticks to a simple daily diet; one-and-a-half pounds of cheese, two loaves of bread, three-quarters of a pound of meat, three pounds of apples and two pounds of oranges washed down by 14 pints of milk. Not surprisingly, Luke – better known to millions of British television viewers as the wrestler Giant Haystacks – lays claim to being one of the country's heaviest men at an incredible hulking weight of 40 stones. At a towering 6 feet 11 inches tall, his vital statistics are equally herculean; his chest measures 76 inches and he has a 64-inch waist. In his size 16 shoes, he stands a truly awesome, bearded figure.

Fantastic fatties like Luke have captured public imagination for centuries. Fat men and women have always been objects of curiosity and a vast number have exhibited themselves for profit. During the last century, nearly every circus and penny museum had its example. Several fat freaks have managed to make a considerable fortune out of their disability. From William the Conqueror, through Henry VIII, Louis XVIII, American President William Taft and Ugundan dictator Idi Amin Dada, fantastic fatties have also risen in public life to positions of enormous power to shape and control the destinies of others.

The fattest man alive today – indeed the heaviest recorded human in medical history – is Jon Brower Minnoch, a 41-year-old former taxi driver from Bainbridge Island, Washington. At times in his life, he has weighed

E. Naucke, born 1855, was reputed to be the biggest man in the world

---

Bonny baby

The bonniest baby ever to bounce into the world must have been tiny titan
James Weir, who tragically died when only thirteen months old in 1821.
According to the headstone on his grave in the Old Parish Cemetery,
Wishaw, Strathclyde, Scotland, he was a staggering 8 stones in weight, 3
feet 4 inches tall and 39 inches in girth.

---

more than 100 stones. During periods of uncontrollable weight gain, he is
claimed to have put on 14 stones in a single week.

Minnoch's unbelievable, ultra roly-poly frame landed him in hospital in
Seattle in 1978, on the brink of death. It took 13 attendants simply to roll him
over in bed. But after 16 months on an emergency crash diet of 1,200 calories
a day, 6 feet 1 inch tall Minnoch was allowed home weighing what for him
was a slimline 34 stones.

His problems still aren't over, however. In October, 1981, he was re-
admitted to Seattle's University Hospital suffering from chronic weight gain
and heart trouble caused by his obesity. The local fire department had to
remove several doors as a 10-man emergency team struggled to get him out of
his home. Doctors have still so far refused to reveal Minnoch's latest weight,
which, at its 100 stone or more peaks can only be estimated by specialists.

America seems to have an image of producing the biggest of everything in
the world – and that applies to fantastic fatties. In fact one city, Durham,
North Carolina, has become the calorie capital of the country and earned
itself the nickname 'Fat City, USA'. It all began 40 years ago, when Doctor
Walter Kempner of Duke University pioneered a revolutionary fruit-and-rice
diet. As waistlines shed inches, the success of his system spread as far and
wide as the stomachs of his patients once did, and fatties from all over
America began to roll into Durham. Today, unhappy fatties who are willing
to pay up to £2,000 for a treatment course have to join a waiting list of 12
months to get into one of the city's four thriving slimming clinics. New York
chef Anthony Milone, who in eight months of hard sweat managed to trim
down from a chair-busting 36 stones 6 pounds to a much more comfortable
23 stones, declared: 'When I first came to Durham, I was so ashamed of the
way I looked that I got up before dawn for a swim so that no-one would see
me. When I went swimming near the end of the course I was the lightest guy
there!'

Other super-fatties who, while not exactly turning into rake-like wraiths,
have managed to slim down to more manageable sizes include an un-named

'Mr Big' who, after tipping the scales at 60 stones, was taken – by hoist – to a New York clinic where doctors, aided by a 15-strong team to move their patient, worked for three hours to cut more than 10 stones from his abdomen. A second operation on the mystery man, who previously had barely been able to walk because of his obesity, succeeded in removing a further 8 stones of flab from his body in October 1981.

It's certainly not rare for man to need mechanical help in lifting fatties. When Robert Earl Hughes from Monticello, Illinois, died, weighing almost half a ton, on 10 July 1958, he set undertakers a formidable task. Eventually, they decided that his coffin, a converted piano case, had to be lowered into its grave by crane. And on 21 July 1809, jovial heavyweight Daniel Lambert caused enormous headaches when he paid his last visit to the Waggon and Horses Inn at Stamford, Lincolnshire, and died in the ground floor bar. A whole wall and the ceiling had to be pulled down before he could be pulled out. Later, it took 20 pall bearers to carry the 52 stone 11 pound Leicester-born Lambert's coffin, which measured 6 feet 4 inches long and 4 feet 4 inches wide.

The only other Briton apart from Lambert to tip the scales at more than 50 stones was Glasgow-born William Campbell, who died, while working as a publican, at the tender age of 22 on 16 June 1878, weighing-in at 53 stones 8 pounds. The heaviest recorded Briton alive today is 47-stone Eric Keeling from Islington, North London. Eleven pounds at birth in 1933, Eric blossomed into an 18-stoner at the age of 13. His peak weight was attained in 1971, when he decided to try to reduce it by dieting. A couple of years later, he had already shrunk to just over 33 stones.

Some fantastic fatties attain such proportions that they actually fit the description 'human cannon-balls', being as wide, if not wider, than they are tall. One such was Mme Marie-Françoise Clay, a French beggar woman who lived during the last century. Although the date is obscured, it is known that at the age of 40, she was 5 feet 1 inch tall and was one inch greater in measurement around the waist. Her breasts were well over a yard in circumference and her arms were permanently elevated and kept away from

Heavy twins

The heaviest twins of all time were Billy and Benny McCrary, of North Carolina, who became professional tag-team wrestlers and bust the scales at a monster weigh-in in November 1978 at 743 pounds and 723 pounds respectively. Both sported 84 inch waists. Tragically, their gargantuan double-act ended in July 1979 when Billy died in a motorcycle accident.

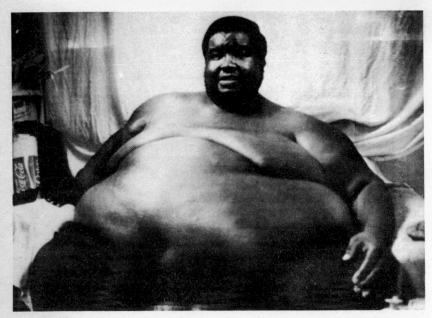

Photographed at a sideshow, Albert weighs 856 pounds

her body by a wall of fat. Astonishingly, she married at the age of 25 and bore six perfectly normal, healthy children. The whole family travelled on foot from village to village, Marie usually augmenting their meagure income from her husband's second-hand clothes barrow by begging at church doors and scavenging what she could. She must have been an incredible sight waddling along behind her husband. It was said that on top of her huge frame was a tiny head – and that her neck was totally obliterated from view by layers of fat.

The heaviest woman who ever lived was Mrs Percy Pearl, who died, aged 46, on 9 October 1972. Before her death, Mrs Pearl had searched long and hard around her home city of Washington for a pair of scales which could actually record her weight; most hospital scales only register up to 800 lbs (57 stones 2 pounds). Eventually though, it was discovered that she easily topped that at a hefty 62 stones 12 pounds. The heaviest-ever British woman was Muriel Hopkins, who registered 43 stones 11 pounds in 1978. Shortly before her death, on 22 April a year later, she had reportedly gone up to 52 stones, but – despite the lack of corroborative evidence – it is estimated, according to the *Guinness Book of Records*, that she more likely scaled around 47½ stones.

Extreme obesity right from the cradle to the grave is not uncommon. Records of super-fat babies reveal the case of a German girl who at birth weighed 13 pounds; at six months, 3 stones; at four years, 10½ stones; and at the age of 20, a toppling 32 stones. A little girl aged only 5½ who was exhibited at a meeting of the Physical Society of Vienna on 4 December 1894, tipped the scales at slightly more than 17 stones. She was just shedding her first teeth, but could only toddle like an infant due to her excess fat. The child, of Russian descent, was said never to perspire and was fed, it said, almost exclusively on cabbage, milk and vegetable soup!

Medical tomes are, indeed, littered with case histories of youngsters – like the 'Tompkins Child' or 'Baby Chambers' – who were born grossly overweight and remained that way through childhood, adolescence and adulthood. The question of whether such obesity is actually congenital still causes debate among leading doctors.

One man who is now single-handedly trying to shed the lifelong layers of fat which at one stage turned him into Cockney East London's celebrated 'King of the Fatties' is 58-year-old social club manager George Macaree, who once merited a Guiness Book of Records entry at a gargantuan 40 stones 4 pounds. George, unlike freak show figures of old who merely showed their bodies for gain, uses his famous frame to raise money for numerous charities, and is already well on his way towards a target of losing half his weight. After a year on a strict 500 calories a day diet, he has shed more than 10 stones so far. Soon he will have to abandon the special armchair which cost £500 to custom-build along with the specially-tailored suits to fit his 84-76-89 figure. But he says: 'I can now tie my own shoelaces whereas before I couldn't even see them. I tried 15 diets before I found the one for me. Now, I'm only allowed three meals a day! It's taken a lot of will power, but I'm proving it can be done.'

Hypnotist Alan Paige is offering other fantastic fatties the sort of cure that the freak show characters of old could never have dreamed of. Alan, from Newcastle, is offering British heavyweights 'fantasy island' package trips to Malta where they can eat and drink all they want, and still come home slimmer. The trick is that it will all be done under hypnosis and Alan, who revealed his tour plan in February 1982, says: 'They will believe they are tucking into steak and chips, when really the meal they will be munching away at is a salad. There's no secret mumbo jumbo about this. Hypnosis is the key.' And, for all fantastic fatties who are still sceptical, he pledges: 'If it doesn't work for any individual, I'll refund the money for the treatment.'

One wonders what Daniel Lambert, Marie-Françoise Clay and a whole heaving host of others would ever have made of that!

No chapter about fantastic fatties could ever be complete without a look at the amazing feats and eats of the world's most gluttonous trenchermen. Perhaps the hungriest of them all has been Edward 'Bozo' Miller, who daily consumes a staggering 25,000 calories.

Bozo, of Oakland, California, who was born in 1909, stands only 5 feet 7½ inches tall but weighs in at anything between 20 to 21½ stones depending on how peckish he's been feeling. He hasn't actually been beaten in an eating contest since 1931 and among his more astonishing feats was the record he established in 1963 by munching his way through 27 small chickens at one sitting.

The same year, Bozo, who boasts a bulging 57-inch waist, also set the world ravioli eating record of 324 with the first 250 swallowed in 70 minutes flat. If wanting to establish gluttony records sounds half-baked to you, don't try giving Peter Dowdswell, of Earls Barton, Northamptonshire, food for thought. He currently holds no less than 14 such records and when it comes to speed-eating he appears to be simply unstoppable.

His records, apart from five for beer and ale, include the following: 1 pound of Cheddar cheese in 1 minute 13 seconds, 1 pound of eels in 13.7 seconds, a 26-ounce haggis in 50 seconds, 22 meat pies in 18 minutes 13 seconds, 2 pints of milk in 3.2 seconds, 62 pancakes in 58.5 seconds, 3 pounds of potatoes in 1 minute 22 seconds, 40 jam sandwiches in 53.9 seconds, 3 pounds of shrimps in 4 minutes 8 seconds, 14 hard-boiled eggs in 58 seconds, 32 soft-boiled eggs in 78 seconds and 13 raw eggs in 2.2 seconds.

Peter would have had another record for prune eating to enter alongside his incredible list in the *Guinness Book of Records*, but for the fact that his time of 78 seconds to eat 144 of them was bettered by 13 seconds in 1978 by Douglas Mein. Generally, the bargees on the Rhine are reckoned to be the world's biggest eaters, averaging around 5,200 calories a day. In December 1972, however, the Federation of Medicine in New Zealand reported an intake of 14,321 calories over a 24-hour period by a long-distance road runner.

The craziest of all eating records must go to a bizarre Frenchman named Lotito, more appropriately nicknamed Monsieur Mangetout (Mr Eat-all) who, in 15 days between 17 March and 2 April 1977, consumed an entire bicycle, eating the frame as metal filings and stewing the tyres!

Records for such voracious eating, and also those for drinking, fail to even begin to compare, however, with the consumption of those people who tragically suffer from the rare disease of bulimia, a morbid desire to eat without stopping, and polydipsia, whose victims endure a pathological thirst. It is not unknown for bulimia sufferers to have to spend anything up to 15 hours solidly eating every day. One of the most extreme cases ever recorded was that of Matthew Daking, then aged only 12, in 1743. In the space of just 6 days he managed to eat an incredible 348 pounds 2 ounces of food.

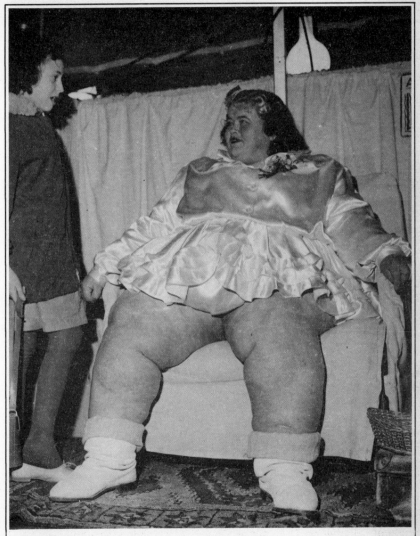

Lydia

Lydia, aged 23, from the Netherlands weighs an astounding 456 pounds. She is pictured here at a Paris fair in 1961.

A man from Johannesburg, Fannie Meyer, was claimed in 1974 to be drinking at least 160 pints of water a day, his incredible thirst apparently and inexplicably the result of a skull fracture. According to a further report four years later, he was managing to slake his thirst with 52 pints a day. Miss Helge Andersson of Lindesberg, Sweden, who was born in 1908, is reported to have drunk 40 pints every day between 1922 and January 1971, an astonishing total of 87,600 gallons during the period.

Hormone deficiencies can also produce unnatural obesity from an early age, producing the sort of 'Fat Boy' freaks who appealed to the Victorians but who lived, in some cases, in constant danger of suffocating themselves to death with their own fat. One such case was that of Carrie Akers, who, though she stood only 34 inches tall, weighed an astonishing 22 stones. And another fat woman, Miss Conley, who belonged to a travelling American circus, actually did smother herself in bed, by rolling onto her face. She was so gigantic that she couldn't turn on her back without help, and, on the night she died, there was nobody around to provide any assistance.

The Victorians discovered a condition, which they called adiposis dolorosa, which coupled gross obesity with other symptoms, such as a recurrent headache, and a painfulness quite different to the sort of discomfort experienced by other people who were simply fat. In one case, a woman whose age was believed to be 38 or 39, was found in June 1887 to be suffering from an inordinate enlargement of her shoulders, arms, back and the sides of her chest. The parts affected by adiposis dolorosa appeared, according to a report, to be elastic. In some places the fat seemed as though it were a writhing mass of worms under skin. Unlike normal cases of obesity, there was no muscular involvement in the condition and the skin was not thickened as it would be in an ordinary fat patient. This remarkable condition was accompanied by great pain whenever an affected area was touched. According to the report, the woman simply appeared to have extremely unsightly wobbling rolls of fat attached to various parts of her body which baffled all medical knowledge.

Little and large

The world's most amazing little and large couple were husband and wife Mills and Mary Darden. He weighed in at a staggering 72 stones 12 pounds, while she barely tipped the scales at a super-slim 7 stones. Despite their differences, it was a case of happy families, though, for Mary is said to have borne her heavyweight husband between three and five children before her death in 1837.

Human Skeletons

In August 1979, a rakish, enfeebled woman from North London shed a few more pounds in weight and died. That month, like many previous months, she had set herself a new slimming target. She considered herself grossly overweight and had been sticking rigidly to a diet of black coffee during the day, a slice of toast or perhaps a small bowl of soup in the evening with a weekly 'treat' of two spoonfuls of potato and maybe, when she felt extra-specially adventurous, a thin slice of cold chicken.

She was 5 feet 3 inches tall yet well under 6 stones in weight when she died, aged 31. In an almost macabre ritual, she had insisted on keeping a detailed diary of her daily fight against imagined flab, often chastising herself for failing to lose a few more pounds and ounces and vowing to eat and drink even less in a pathetic effort to be perfectly thin.

In Britain alone, one in every 200 adolescent girls suffers at some stage from the perplexing syndrome which killed that woman: anorexia nervosa, or, as it has more popularly come to be known, 'slimmers' disease'. The figure is twice as high for girls aged 16 or more who are at university or in private higher education. The stark medical fact is that 15 out of every 100 sufferers will dies, 35 will endure relapses and only 50 – half the total – will completely recover.

Slimmers' disease is far removed from the Victorian peep show world of the human skeleton; instead, psychologists believe, it is an aberration of 20th century life's intense peer-group and media pressure on women, and especially teenage girls, to slim and slim again, to stay young and beautiful and so not only attract the opposite sex but also, though it is never explained quite why, become a better person.

Young girls, battered by glossy advertisements and myriad slimming guides, have been known to suffer incredible and sometimes lethal weight losses as they take crash diets to dangerous extremes, each lost pound fuelling the belief that they can and must lose more. Models, film stars and pop singers have been categorized as high risk professions and there are literally hundreds of cases of women in these fields who, before the constant gaze of the public, have fallen victim to anorexia.

One famous personality, who became consumed with a desire to cut her intake of food to bare subsistence level to achieve what she believed would be a ravishing hour-glass figure, starved herself virtually to the brink of death. The efforts of doctors, a long period recuperation in a private clinic and help from a leading psychiatrist eventually broke her obsessive need to fast.

There are few genuine human skeletons who enjoy good health along with their lean times. Many of the freaks exhibited in Victorian England and across America did, in fact suffer from acute muscular atrophy; their withered, limp limbs but perfectly normal, adult-sized heads often giving them the appearance of being grotesquely shaped dwarfs. One such tragic figure was a woman called Rosa Lee Plemons, whose hideously atrophied body weighed only 27 pounds when she was 18-years-old.

Perhaps the most celebrated human skeleton was a little Welshman named Hopkin Hopkins, who never weighed more than 17 pounds during his life as a freak on show in his native country and in London. In the three years prior to his death in Glamorganshire in March 1754, at the age of 17, his weight had remained at a static 12 pounds. It is believed that he suffered from precocious development, that rare and cruel disease that causes the ageing process of youngsters to speed out of control until they die, pitifully, of old age before they are out of their teens. Hopkin Hopkins' parents had six other children, all of whom were of sound health apart from a 12-year-old sister, who weighed a mere 18 pounds and was showing signs of beginning to wither and age rapidly on the death of her brother.

In total contrast, J. W. Coffey, who became a hugely successful star on the peep show circuit, became known as – and, indeed, lived like – the 'King of the Human Skeletons'. He was renowned among his friends and showbusiness colleagues as a voracious eater whose hefty appetite startled men many times his weight. Despite his skeletal stature – his bones and joints were clearly visible jutting out under taut, seemingly elasticated skin – he was known always to enjoy superb health and his jolly demeanour, which would have been more appropriate perhaps to one of the roly-poly fatties whom human skeletons were often staged alongside, became the talk of Victorian voyeurs who flocked to see him at circuses and penny museums throughout the country.

Cannibalism

Cannibalism is, thankfully, extremely rare nowadays. But it was rife in many places right until the beginning of this century. Apparently the most voracious eaters of human flesh were some Maoris in New Zealand who – unlike their Antipodean cousins in Australia who preferred to munch their way through dead relatives – were quite undiscerning about who ended up on their dinner table! As many as 1,000 prisoners at one time are said to have been baked in underground ovens and eaten by 19th century New Zealanders.

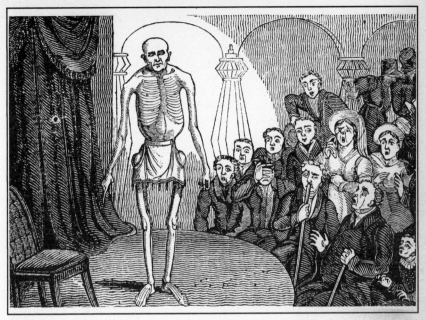

Claude Seurat, born in 1798

Another human skeleton, who was brought to England in 1825, certainly didn't share his contemporary's appetite for plentiful fare. Frenchman Claude Seurat's humble daily diet consisted of a meagre penny roll and a few thimble-sized sips of wine. Seurat, who was born in 1798 and so did not hit the lucrative freak scene in England until he was 27 years old, had truly astonishing physical dimensions. The distance from his chest to his spine – measured, of course, from the outside of his body – was only 3 inches. The circumference of his biceps was a mere 4 inches and, with his skeletal frame plainly visible under his tightly-stretched skin, peep show customers were alarmed, amused and amazed actually to *see* his heartbeats!

Seurat's voice was said to have been incredibly weak and shrill and he was, of course, a very feeble man. Yet he enjoyed perfect health all his life, despite his miniscule daily intake of sustenance, slept well and, according to doctors who observed him, seemed not in the least worried about his frailty and had no desire to be helped or improved by being fattened-up.

American soldier Calvin Edson, who served as a 25-year-old trooper in 1813 at the battle of Plattsburg during the war against the British, became famous as a human skeleton in a bizarre way. After the long and bloody battle, fought in bitterly cold conditions, he simply collapsed, completely exhausted and numb from the appalling weather. At the time, he was a healthy 125 pounds. But, almost instantly and for no apparent reason, he began to lose weight alarmingly. No matter what he did or ate, he could not arrest the amazing automatic diet. Seventeen years after the battle his weight had more than halved to a scant 60 pounds. Yet no matter how lightly he tipped the scales, he retained his strength and perfect health. By 1830, Edson, who was by then a father of four, could chop huge piles of wood, despite the fact that his 5 feet 4 inches height carried just a bundle of flesh and bones.

The lightest ever human being on record was Lucia Zarate, who weighed 2½ pounds at her birth in San Carlos, Mexico, on January 2, 1863. By her seventeenth birthday, she had gained only another 2 pounds in weight! The emaciated girl, who was also a dwarf who stood only 26½ inches high, actually began to fill out a little more after that – by her 20th birthday she was pleased to be tipping the scales at 13 pounds! Lucia's frail little life came to an end in October 1889, when she died at the age of 26, still weighing only 13 pounds.

Bag-of-bones freaks enjoyed great success and had huge followings during the heyday of the peep show and were often exhibited under such spectacular and quasi-medical sounding names as 'The Ossified Man'. Edward C. Hagner, who was born in America and lived from 1892 to 1962, relished his Wild West-style handle of 'The Skeleton Dude'. Standing 5 feet 7 inches high, he is said to have weighed at his peak a paltry 3 stones 6 pounds of skin and bones.

Rare diseases are known to have caused staggering losses of up to 65 per cent of body weight in people. The shrunken frame of Emma Shaller, who was born in St Louis, Missouri, on 8 July 1868 and died 22 years later, weighed only 3 stones 3 pounds. Emma, who stood 5 feet 2 inches tall, had been of average weight for her height until she contracted the extremely rare disease Hypophysial cachexia – known also as Simmonds' disease. Like anorexia nervosa the disease causes rapid weight loss, often over a very short period.

Today it would be callous and unimaginable to seek to exploit as human skeletons and freaks the many hundreds of thousands of emaciated little figures which have touched the consciences of us all: grief-stricken figures with no food for their bellies who are the children of the Third World. Since the flood of pictures of skeletal Biafran infants began to flow in the 1960s into the torrent from Vietnam, Kampuchea and elsewhere, this subject which may have caused so much mawkish pleasure in the days of showpiece Victoriana at its best, now perhaps evokes feelings closer to the heart.

Strongmen

From Samson to Sandow to the children's fantasy character of the Incredible Hulk, now immortalized by television, feats of mighty muscular power by strong men and women have always fascinated us more feeble mortals.

Today's Olympic weight and power-lifters captivate TV audiences of millions with the jerks, squats and snatches that can raise loads in excess of five hundredweight. Circus strong-men still thrive in an era in which human competition rather than the mere display of freakish prowess is all-important.

Had Scotsman Angus Macaskill lived in the 20th century, he would undoubtedly have been among the leading contenders for that most elusive, often challenged and more often unofficially claimed title of the strongest man the world has ever seen. Born in the Outer Hebrides in 1825, he grew to be a giant of a man, standing 7 feet 9 inches tall in bare feet and with physical abilities to match.

Signed up in later life by the showman Barnum, he spent his early days as a dock worker-cum-fisherman. It is said that he could raise the mast of a fishing boat with one hand and was able to throw hundredweight sacks from the bottom of a boat right up onto the jetty with consummate ease. On a voyage to Nova Scotia, startled bystanders witnessed him carrying an enormous ship's anchor over one shoulder – a feat which is boldly recorded in the *Guinness Book of Amazing People* as 'the heaviest weight ever carried by a human being'.

Despite his enormous power, however, Macaskill was known as a gentle giant who steered well clear of public brawls and was shy of demonstrating his strength. When the champion heavyweight wrestler of Canada tried to provoke a fight with him, Macaskill decided that the only was he could avoid killing the man was to insist on shaking hands. As he gripped the Canadian's palm in a 'friendly' gesture, the wrestler's eyes began to bulge as he saw blood

---

Convict strongman

Prison exercise did Austrian convict Joseph Pospischilli a power of good. During incarceration in the fortress jail of Olen in the 19th century, he astonished his captors by balancing two gipsy dancers on a huge table with his teeth. When freed, he became a strong-man entertainer, earning a fortune touring southern Europe.

John Topham

Heaviest-ever

Twenty-five stone Olympic and professional weightlifter Paul Anderson, of Toccoa, Georgia, who became known as 'The Dixie Derrick', claimed the title of raising the heaviest weight ever lifted by a man on 12 June 1957, when he hoisted aloft an almost unbelievable 6,270 pounds on his back. The weight is the equivalent of two family saloon cars, or three entire football teams.

---

oozing from under his fingernails. Macaskill simply smiled politely and the stunned wrestler happily accepted his chance to back down.

The giant Scotsman was so strong that the incorrigible Barnum not only exhibited him, but also set him to work erecting big top tents. Macaskill used a 14-pound hammer – in *each* hand – to drive home the stakes. Other circus owners did their best to woo him away from Barnum and persuade him to become an all-in wrestler. But quietly-spoken Macaskill was content to stay where he was, doing the work of a dozen men for one man's wage!

Word of his Herculean feats in the Barnum shows was quickly picked up by royal freak enthusiast Queen Victoria, who summoned the Scottish Samson to Windsor Castle. The shy strong-man was so nervous at the prospect of meeting and amusing Her Majesty – who was almost three feet shorter than he – that he damaged the castle carpets by shuffling his huge feet. What did the damage were the two horseshoes he had welded on to the bottom of his boots!

Great strong-men throughout history have pitted their power against animals, cars, trains and supposedly immovable objects in incredible 'tug o' war' matches. 19th century Londoner Thomas Topham regularly won such matches using his teeth alone . . . against two horses!

Topham, who stood a mere 5 feet 10 inches tall, could also lift, and hold in a horizontal position, a 6-foot long table – again using just his teeth. Holding a bit between those mighty molars, Topham's only real failure came when he lost yet another tug o' war, this time against four horses. He more than compensated for that, however, by turning to a different but equally exacting act – carrying a gigantic rolling pin, weighing 800 pounds, in his hands.

Another celebrated Victorian strong-man was Tom Johnson, a porter on the banks of the Thames who once doubled his workload by carrying out the duties of a sick colleague who could not provide for his wife and family. Johnson's job was to carry sacks of wheat and corn from the wharves to warehouses, and he was said to be so adept at carrying them that he could actually hurl them for several yards using the actions of a club-swinger.

When Johnson heard that the porters of Paris were used to carrying bags of flour weighing 350 pounds over their shoulders, he determined to outdo them three times over. Very soon he was able to carry three such sacks, with a combined weight of over 1,000 pounds over his shoulders with no apparent discomfort.

A more recent show of super-strength was that demonstrated by 40-year-old Belgian beefcake John Massis. On 19 October 1976, he must have shocked the world's dentists when, with his teeth alone, he pulled a British Rail locomotive and truck, together weighing an incredible 121 tons, along a level track at Park Royal, London. With the bit firmly between his teeth, he repeated the feat in Sweden two years later, this time pulling three railway carriages.

Massis can bend metal bars, bite enormous nails out of wooden blocks and lift a Fiat car into the air using only a harness attached to his jaws. He has lifted a staggering weight of 513 pounds from the ground with his teeth. But his most amazing stunt must have been the one he performed in front of television cameras in Los Angeles in 1979. Using only a bit between his teeth attached to a harness, he managed to prevent a helicopter from taking off.

Punjabi taxi driver Tara Chand Saggar is another modern-day master of muscle-power. And, like Samson, he claims that his enormous power comes from his long hair. In May 1972 at the age of 72 he decided to prove it. He walked into the offices of a Calcutta newspaper and, using a series of ropes to attach a board to his curly, brown locks, managed to lift a burly printer, weighing 143 pounds, a foot off the floor, using hair-power only.

Unfortunately, the rope knots gave way, and the recoil almost flung Saggar out of the office window. He apologized for the mishap and promised to return when his hair was longer and stronger. He did just that, barely two weeks later, and repeated the feat with total success, this time lifting a 165-pound printer off the ground!

Strongwomen

One claim to being the world's strongest-ever woman was made by 5 feet 11 inches tall Katie Sandwina, a housewife who found fame in John Ringling's freak circus in the early 1900s. Quite apart from making mincemeat of a 286-pound load in 1911 – which is recorded as the greatest overhead lift ever made by a woman – she also showed her strength

Katie Sandwina

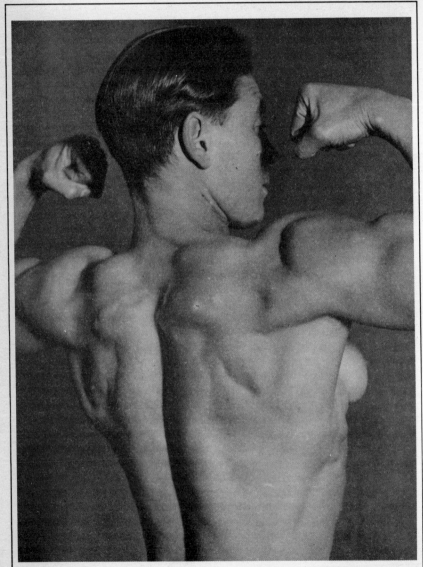

Ivy, photographed in 1930, was a champion wrestler and could lift a grand piano

by carrying a 1,200-pound cannon on her shoulder and performing military rifle exercises, using her 160-pound husband Max instead of a rifle!

The record for the greatest weight actually lifted by a woman belongs to Mrs Josephine Blatt, who raised an astonishing 3,564 pounds on her broad shoulders at the Bijou Theatre, Hoboken, New Jersey, on 13 April 1895. Among other famous strong women, from the period when freak shows were at the height of popularity, were the Frenchwoman Madame Elise and Miss Darnett, an English girl who became known as 'The Singing Stronglady'.

Madame Elise, who performed with her husband, was capable of lifting eight men with a combined weight of roughly 1,700 pounds. Miss Darnett, doing a back arch on the floor, could play the piano and sing while a platform, laden with a half-ton weight, was balanced on her chest, abdomen and thighs.

Acknowledgements

To complete a book such as this, the author must draw much of his inspiration and information from earlier works. It would be impossible to list them all, but the author wishes, in particular, to acknowledge the following:

George M. Gould, AM, MD, and Walter L. Pyle, AM, MD, *Anomalies and Curiosities of Medicine* (W. B. Saunders 1896); Leslie Fiedler, *Freaks – Myths and Images of the Secret Self* (Penguin 1981); Martin Howard, *Victorian Grotesque* (Jupiter 1977) ; Daniel Farson and Angus Hall, *Great Mysteries, Mysterious Monsters* (Aldus 1975); Norris McWhirter, editor, *Guinness Book of Records* (Guiness Superlatives 1982); Shirley Greenway, editor, *The Guinness Book of Amazing People* (Piccolo 1981); Michael Howell and Peter Ford; *The True History of the Elephant Man* (Penguin 1980); Jules Romains; *Eyeless Sight* (Citadel Press 1978); and the following newspapers and magazines; in London: *The Lancet*; *The British Medical Journal*; *John Bull*; *The Times*; *The Daily Telegraph*; *News of the World*; *The Sun*; *Daily Mirror*; *Daily Express*; *Daily Star*; *Daily Mail*; *Evening News* (now defunct); in the USA: *National Enquirer*; *Weekly World News*; *Globe*; *New York Times*; *Washington Post*.

The publishers wish to thank the following individuals and organisations for their kind permission to reproduce the photographs in this book:

Camera Press 89, 120, Circus World 68, Daily Star Picture Library 41, Mary Evans Picture Library 38, 49, 65, 77 above, 79, 90, 93, 94, 117, 156, 166, 169 above, 183, Fortena Picture Library 63, The Mansell Collection 60, 163, 173, 186, 190, Radio Times Hulton Picture Library 2, 6, 17, 27, 31, 35, 43, 77 below, 81, 97, 109, 153, 169, 171, 189, Syndication International 129, John Topham Picture Library 11, 13, 106, 127, 133, 141, 145, 176, 179, Wide World Photographs Inc. 20.